MAKING
YOUR
52
DAILY
READS

How to READ the Defense of your Opponents' Objections to Christianity and Make the Right Call to Uphold the Faith

Do You Have a Ready Answer for These Questions from Non-Christians?

R One **religion** is as good as another

E **Editing** God's Word to fit our presuppositions

A **Apologetics**: defending the faith against common objections

D God is **dead** when it comes to "real life" issues

S The **State** is exempt from God's authority

Buddy Hanson

Brandon—

"The sons of this world are more shrewd in their generation than the sons of light."

Luke 16.8

Buddy

Scripture quotations are from the New Geneva Study Bible,
NKJV, 1995, Thomas Nelson, Inc.

© 2008 Hanson Group
2 Windsor Drive • Tuscaloosa, Alabama 35404
205.454.1442
bhanson@graceandlaw.com • www.graceandlaw.com
ISBN-0-9771773-8-6
Printed and bound in the United States of America

MAKING YOUR 52 DAILY READS

AUDIBLE R
One **Religion** is as Good as Another

WEEK 1

WEEK 2

WEEK 3

AUDIBLE E
Editing God's Word to Fit our Presuppositions

AUDIBLE A
Apologetics: Defending the Faith against Common Objections

AUDIBLE D
God is **Dead** When it Comes to "Real Life" Issues

AUDIBLE S
The **State** is Exempt from God's Authority

WEEK 51

WEEK 52

PREFACE

WHAT IN THE WORLD IS THIS BOOK ALL ABOUT? IS IT A SPORTS BOOK? NO, BUT it will appeal to Christian sports fans of all ages. Then, why does the cover reflect a football theme, and use a football phrase for the title? Unfortunately many of our Christian brothers and sisters know a lot more about their favorite sports team and their vocation than they know about how the Bible instructs them to live and govern themselves. When they watch their favorite team, they are much more savvy about what play a particular situation calls for, than they are about what Christian response a particular situation or circumstance in their everyday decision-making calls for.

Deep down, each of us knows this shouldn't be the case. In the recesses of our mind we know that we shouldn't be more knowledgeable or passionate about a game than we are about our life. Sadly, many pastors contribute to this problem, rather than assisting us in solving it, by stopping their instruction with what the Bible says, instead of including how to incorporate biblical truths into our worldview and lifestyle. We also know that even though we deserve much more from our pastors, we can't use their hesitancy to preach and teach the whole counsel of God as an excuse for not conforming our lifestyle to biblical principles.

However, it is at this point that many of us are overwhelmed at the prospect of presenting a consistent day-to-day Christian antithesis to our non-Christian neighbors. Simply put, we don't know where to start or how to begin the process by which we can grow in God's grace and knowledge.

> *If this describes you, take a breath because you have just opened the pages to a process by which you, your family and children can incrementally increase your knowledge of the fundamental basics of Christianity.*

The format and presentation of *Making Your 52 Daily READS* is designed to under whelm you with its simple and easy to follow process of preparing you to bring honor to Jesus in all you think, say and do. In the first place there is only one page for you to read and think about for an entire week! So this overcomes the problem of not being able to fit a daily Quiet Time (or Daily Spiritual Practice, see Appendix Two) into one's schedule. In the second place the IN YOUR OWN WORDS page gives you a model upon which you can build your response along with some suggested questions to use in talking with non-Christians. These questions are designed to assist them in seeing the foolishness of their objections to Christianity.

For those who are thinking, "This sounds good, but I have so much to learn that I don't want to limit myself to only one biblical concept per week," let me ask you this: "How many biblical concepts did you learn last week, or the week before that, or the week before that?" Rather than having the good intentions of quickly accelerating your Christian growth, but never seeming to know how to begin the process, wouldn't it be much better to repetitively and thoroughly train yourself in one principle per week, so that you will be so familiar with it that you will have a ready answer for your non-Christian friends for the rest of your life?

If you agree, then *Making Your 52 Daily READS* is exactly what you have been praying for.

Buddy Hanson
Tuscaloosa, Alabama

Introduction

THE WRITER OF THE BOOK OF HEBREWS TELLS US GOD'S WORD "IS SHARPER than any two-edged sword," [1] and the apostle Paul says it "thoroughly equips us for every good work." [2] So when we begin the process of building answers to the common objections we often encounter, our first stop should be God's Word! Indeed, it is precisely because someone does not know God's Word, or has misunderstood it that we hear objections, such as:

R   It's not fair for non-Christian nations to be held accountable to God's Laws, because they don't know what His Laws are!

E   Why bother trying to improve the world. Aren't we living in the "last days?"

A   How could your God be "loving," and still send sinners to Hell?

D   As a preacher, I should not teach about cultural issues.

S   The state doesn't have to keep the civil laws of the Bible since modern nations are not in covenant with God.

The purpose of these 52 Daily Reads is to assist you in building your answers, in your own words. We know that Paul instructs us to have an answer "in season, and out-of-season," [3] but this is one of those truths we tend to suppress because we think, "Man, I'd have to be a walking encyclopedia to have answers ready for every objection!" My response to that would be: "Not if you put them into categories." By doing this, even if you hear an objection for the first time you can mentally sort it into the proper category and voila, you'll have an answer (even though it may be a generic one and not a specific one). Another advantage you have in defending the faith is that the way people think has not changed over the years. Today, we are certainly more technologically advanced than at any time in the past, but we still use the same processes of thinking. So the correct answer to a question about Christianity in the 1600s would still be correct today. Of course you would probably want to substitute some of the "thees," and "thous" for modern English, but the content would remain the same. The advantage this gives you is that the types of objections you will occasionally run up against are predictable! You may not know when you will encounter a particular objection, but you can be confident that there are only so many types of objections you will encounter.

This is why the Daily Reads are grouped in five categories under the title, Audibles. Taken together, the individual letters representing the Audible make up the acronym

"READS" a football term that refers to the quarterback "reading" the defensive alignment as he comes to the line of scrimmage. For example, if he comes to the line with a running play and notices that the defense has eight men within five yards of the line of scrimmage, he will realize that there are too many defenders for his linemen to block, which also means that there will be too few defenders to play the pass, so he should "audible" out of the running play and into a passing play.

Obviously, it wouldn't do the quarterback any good to do this if he and his teammates hadn't spent time in practice on various passing and running plays. This is what *Making Your Daily READS* is all about…giving you "practice time" against the various "defenses" you come face-to-face with each morning when you step outside the friendly confines of your home.

Each section begins with a listing of the Audibles. Each Audible begins with a concise, one-page Scouting Report that outlines some fundamental characteristics of a Christian worldview, plus basic points that can be used successfully against the non-Christian objections that are discussed in that section. These will help get your thoughts established according to the topics that are discussed. As a bonus, a short course in apologetics, entitled "Five Biblical Principles I may Encounter Today!" is included in Appendix One.

While *Making Your Daily READS* will appeal to football fans of all ages, it is not necessary to know anything about football in order to benefit from the valuable insights and helpful suggestions about preparing yourself to be ready "in season and out" to "defend the faith."

Audibles

As mentioned, the audibles are arranged topically according to the acronym READS, which stands for:

R One **religion** is as good as another
E **Editing** God's Word to fit our presuppositions
A **Apologetics**; defending the faith against common objections
D God is **dead** when it comes to "real life" issues.
S The **State** is exempt from God's authority.

The plan is simple. Each week covers one topic, so that each day you are clarifying and mentally reinforcing your understanding of the foolishness of one aspect of the non-Christian worldview. Spending an entire week on one of the READS will help you to build your response in your own words so that you will be ready for whatever misinformation and/or misguided objections you encounter in your daily duties.*

---

* *"Duties" is used, instead of "routine" because living the Christian life is far from routine!*

A MODEL FOR "THAWING THE ICE" OF A NON-CHRISTIAN'S HEART

How to Use the "IN YOUR OWN WORDS" Page

The acronym ICE can be used as an effective model in contrasting non-Christian worldview principles with Christian principles. The I stands for the *issue* summarized ("What do you mean by that?"). The C stands for *clarifying* the religion or worldview associated with it ("What is the worldview, and/or the authority which supports your view? Are you willing to base your eternal destiny upon your view?"). The E stands for *exposing* it for the self-contradicting foolishness that it is. The ultimate consequences of the non-Christian worldview present a clear and consistent record of failure throughout history. When this is contrasted with the historical record of success of communities, states, and nations who have followed Christian principles, the non-Christian should be challenged to re-consider the basic presuppositions upon which his worldview is based. It should also be pointed out that the successful Christian worldview is based upon four God-appointed self-governing spheres, which foster personal liberty and freedom, as opposed to the central governing principles of the non-Christian worldview, which foster tyranny and a loss of personal freedom. Point out to your non-Christian neighbors the basic responsibilities of each God-ordained self-governing sphere (individual, family, church, state), and explain which self-governing sphere(s) should be handling the particular issue under discussion. The following statement may sound a little arrogant or cocky, but it isn't intended to be. It is critically important to remember who you are.

> *You have been mercifully and graciously called out of the intellectual stupor in which you were born and given the Holy Spirit to guide you into the truth! Christians are the only people on the face of the earth who know the truth.*

So by acting in conformity to Biblical principles we are going to sooner or later demonstrate our God's wisdom. In like manner, non-Christians are going to sooner or later demonstrate their foolishness, because they are acting according to error.

Again, I state this not out of pride, but out of humility, because even though we have the "truth," we didn't discover it, it was revealed to us. Otherwise we would still be like our non-Christian neighbors who think they have the truth, but whose paths, if not repented of, lead to death and eternal agony. In the meantime, you can be confident that any objection you encounter will have built-in contradictions, because that's all they have. So be a good listener and if at first you don't see the contradiction, ask clarifying questions to keep them talking and sooner or later the contradiction will become apparent, and you will be able to use it in building your answer.

The IN YOUR OWN WORDS page provides space for you to write the KeyPoints to incorporate in your answer to questions and/or objections from non-Christians. Following this are some suggested questions you can use to keep the conversation going, plus keep it directed at the objective truths contained in God's Word, instead of the subjective feelings and emotions that are at the bottom of non-Christian comments.

The ICE Acronym

Issue summarized ("What do you mean by that?")

Clarify the religion associated with it (worldview/authority "Are you willing to base your eternal destiny upon your view?")

Expose it for the self-contradicting foolishness that it is.

- Contrast its ultimate consequences (a consistent record of failure throughout history) with (the historic record of success of communities, states and nations who have followed) Christian principles.
- Explain which self-governing sphere(s) should be handling the issue.

Why Were These Topics Selected?

Making Your Daily READS is written to be a resource for people who are already Christians. It is a "playbook" on how to live the various aspects of the Christian life, rather than a "how to" book on becoming a Christian. To use our football analogy, when the offensive team goes into the huddle between plays they are not discussing how to perform a particular play, but rather which play to use. They are already football players, or else they would be spectators and not on the field of play.

As you well know, Christianity is not a "spectator sport." Each of us has been called out of the self-centered spiritual darkness in which we were born and illuminated by the Holy Spirit to correctly understand how to live and govern ourselves so that we can bring glory and honor to God in everything we say and do. It is impossible to be "salt and light" to our non-Christian neighbors by "sitting in the stands" and simply watching life unfold, as non-Christians run up and down our cultural landscape.[4] Neither can we expect to fulfill Christ's command to "disciple the nations" unless we get onto the "field of play."[5]

The topics presented in *Making Your Daily READS* are designed to assist you in "how to live" your Christian life, rather than "how to obtain" the Christian life. While there is a profundity of books and sermons explaining how to become a Christian, there is a paucity of information on how to live the Christian life. It is my hope that *Making Your Daily READS* helps fill that gap.

Is There Life After "Life?"

You've just completed a new members class at your church and are standing with the other new members at the front of the sanctuary at the conclusion of the worship service. What would be your reaction if one member after another came up to give you the "right hand of fellowship" and said,

> *Welcome to the 'Club!' Now that you're 'in', you are on your own to figure out how to live your life. It's nice meeting you. I look forward to seeing you next Sunday. If you will excuse me, I have to meet the other new members!*

Wow! I don't know what your reaction would be to such a statement, but mine would be something to the effect of "What in the world is being a Christian all about?! How should I and the other new members go about 'figuring out how to live' as Christians?" While I would hope that no new Christian would ever be greeted with such a cold and indifferent statement, the unfortunate truth is that a church that systematically and diligently instructs its members (new and old) in how to live the Christian life is rare. This is not to say that over the course of years in a church a member won't get an abundance of teaching on the "what" of the Bible, but for a variety of reasons (all unbiblical), few church officers instruct the "how" of the Bible.

As Christians, we have no doubt that there is "life after death." Indeed, there is eternal life, either in joyful fellowship with Christians and our triune God in heaven, or in everlasting and excruciating torment with non-Christians and Satan in hell. A question that might prove difficult for many of us to answer is:

Is there a "new way of living" after we receive our "new life?"

If a non-Christian visited a congregational meeting in your church and asked "How does the worldview and lifestyles of your members differ from my lifestyle?" what would you and your fellow members answer? What "examples" could be cited from your worldview and lifestyle that testify that you are, indeed, a Christian? If all you and fellow members could come up with is "we're nicer," or "more polite," or "more moral," then, according to God's Word, you would fail the exam.

Every Christian knows that our worldview and lifestyle should be different than non-Christians, yet the emphasis in most churches is on doing all we can to evangelize our non-Christian neighbors with little or no emphasis on discipling them once they make a profession of faith. With this being the case, why should we expect there to be any significant difference in our "new life" and our "old life?" It's as though once we joyfully welcome a brother or sister into Christ's Kingdom we can think of nothing else to say than "Now that you're in our Christian club, it's up to you to figure out what you're supposed to do from here on out, because we don't have any rules, since we live by 'grace,' and not 'law.'"

Jesus does not present the Christian life as being one whereby we either "sink or swim." As we know, there's a third option to this misguided approach to Christianity: Without clear and explicit training in how to live God-honoring lives the vast majority of our brothers and sisters

> Since the "weeks" are not dated, you can begin *Making Your Daily READS* at anytime!

have learned to "swim poorly." *Making Your Daily READS* is designed to assist you in becoming a world conquering swimmer. At times you may find yourself swimming upstream and/or in some very choppy cultural waters, but in those instances you have the confidence of having Christ's lifejacket to buoy you and His Word to keep you on course.

The Importance of Carrying out Your Assignments

You're a defensive back and the clock is running down in the fourth quarter. The game is tied and the opposing team is methodically marching down the field for the winning score. All of a sudden they complete a pass to their tight end who weighs about 50 pounds more than you and he's running straight in your direction. What do you do? Even if you tackle him, he's already made a first down and they will be on the 10 yard line and in perfect position to run out the clock and kick a winning field goal. Do you carry out your assignment and tackle him, and risk a possible injury since he's so much bigger than you (even though they will be able to have an almost certain field goal), or do you take a wrong angle and let him go into the end zone?

All year long and even before the season began, your coaches have emphasized the importance of each player carrying out his assignments, because if that is done, the results will take care of themselves. You know that your coaches are right, so you remain faithful to them and carry out your assignment by tackling the big tight end as hard as you can. This causes him to fumble the ball out of the end zone, giving your team the ball on your 20 yard line. On the ensuing possession your quarterback completes a long pass to put your team in position to win the game with a field goal. Your faithful allegiance to your coaches proves them right. Good things do happen when you carry out your assignments!

In the Christian life, we rely on the Creator of the universe to bring our obedience into conformity to His eternally perfect plan for the earth! In some instances, it is easier to be obedient than in others, but in all instances we must not forget that Jesus is in complete control of His creation and therein lies our hope and confidence. It is not our responsibility to try to figure out how our obedience can result in positive changes to our culture. That's His job. Our job is to obey Him by faithfully and consistently carrying out our assignments each day and then trusting-in and relying upon Him to "bring about His will on earth as it is in heaven"[6] according to His eternally perfect plans.

To Live For

Everyone is religious and everyone worships their god (even if their "god" is themselves). For the vast majority of people, a belief in their god equates to a positive hope for where they will spend eternity. Religion for them is something to "die for."

Christianity, however, is different. While it is true that our eternal life in heaven with all the other saints, will be a time of indescribable joy, our temporary life on earth is also supposed to be far superior to the lifestyle of a non-Christian. In the first place, we have been mercifully called out of spiritual darkness and into God's marvelous light in order to "subdue and rule over" creation.[7] We know that we are special creatures of God, which means that we know who we are. We are also commanded to "disciple the nations,"[8] and to bring about God the Father's will "on earth as it is in heaven,"[9] which means that we know what we're supposed to do. We also know that God's will for the earth will be brought about through four self-governing spheres of the individual, family, church and state, which means we know how we're supposed to live and govern ourselves.

> ## *Only* Christians Have These Key Ingredients to Life!
>
> *WE KNOW*
> - Who we are
> - What we're supposed to do, and
> - How we're supposed to do it.

Knowing these three key ingredients of life gives us meaning, purpose, and direction. Non-Christians have none of these answers. All they have is their false, self-serving and self-deceiving opinions and delusions and since they don't believe in absolute truth, they can't look to history in order to learn whether such ideas have met with success or failure. This means that while we can learn the lessons of history, they have to experience them! All-in-all, we have a true religion to "live for, *and* die for," while they have a false religion that only offers satisfaction if they "die" for it. This having been said, the question we must ask ourselves is:

 Does my worldview and lifestyle reflect that Christianity only offers advantages in the "hereafter?"

If it does, we need to make some changes in our behavior, because in one way or another, we are coming up short in realizing the meaningful and enjoyable life that Christ intends us to have.

Take a sheet of paper and draw a vertical line down the center of it. On left side write "Christian worldview" and on the right write "Non-Christian worldview." Then make a list of what you consider to be the advantages of each worldview. For illustrative purposes, only list the advantages of each view with regards to life on the earth. And only list those advantages that are reflected in your lifestyle. CAUTION: You will be tempted to list some Christian advantages that are in the Bible, but not in your worldview or lifestyle. If you decide to list them, place an asterisk beside them, indicating that you are going to begin to incorporate them into your lifestyle, or if you want to really shock yourself, don't list them at all.

After you complete your list of Christian and non-Christian earthly advantages, compare them and see how different your worldview and lifestyle is from that of non-Christians. If there a great difference, congratulate yourself on having a developed Christian worldview. If there is a small difference, determine how you can incorporate some of your listed items with an asterisk into your lifestyle. If there is no difference, REPENT and get serious about your Christian walk!

WORLDVIEW AND LIFESTYLE
TROUBLE-SHOOTING SUGGESTIONS

SUGGESTION ONE: Non-Christians view their religion as being an important, but not an integral part of their worldview and lifestyle. To their way of thinking religion is something they "add" to their lifestyle in order to make them a better person. To the contrary, Christianity is a complete transformation of one's worldview and lifestyle. It doesn't usually happen overnight, but rather is a gradual transformation throughout the person's lifetime.

? *How different is your worldview and lifestyle now than it was before you became a Christian?*

? *Do you view Christianity as an "add-on" or a "complete transformation" to your lifestyle?*

SUGGESTION TWO: Since non-Christians place the primary importance of their "god" in the afterlife they make daily decisions according to their own wisdom and resources. Christianity, on the other hand, acknowledges God as being all-knowing and man's reasoning as being negatively affected by Adam and Eve's sin, which means that Christians strive to re-think God's revealed truths and conform their decisions and actions accordingly. How about you?

? *Are you tempted to "help God out" with your wisdom in certain decisions, rather than living in strict conformity of His Word?*

SUGGESTION THREE: Non-Christians depend upon the state to educate their children, provide their health care and govern their lifestyles. By contrast, Christians carry out God's will on earth through four self-governing spheres of the individual, family, church and state.

? *As a Christian are you depending upon central government or self-government?*

SUGGESTION FOUR: Non-Christians see life as being made up of two realms: religion and real life. They believe that people are free to believe in whatever "god" they want, as long as they don't bring their religious beliefs into the real life realm. Christians, in direct antithesis to this, (should!) believe that God created a universe, not a biverse, [10] and that since He created all things and all people, there is not a square inch of His creation that is not to be governed according to His revealed Word.

? *Are you guilty of only thinking about biblical principles when you are at church or in a Bible study?*

SUGGESTION FIVE: With our culture rapidly devolving into rampant non-Christian ethics,

? *Do you believe the reasons for it can be directly tied to Christians being guilty of not making the biblically correct decisions described in these TROUBLESHOOTING SUGGESTIONS?*

? *Can you think of possible additional reasons? If so,*

? *What's stopping you from incorporating these "Godly solutions" into your worldview and lifestyle and then trusting-in and relying-upon the triune God of Scripture to bless the efforts of you and fellow Christians throughout America?*

Christianity is the only true religion and is therefore the only religion worth "living for." Let's get busy doing just that and make Satan's worst nightmare come true by subduing and ruling over the earth!

> *As each one has received a gift, minister it to one another, as good stewards of the manifold grace of God. If anyone speaks, let him speak as the oracles of God. If anyone ministers, let him do it as with the ability which God supplies, that in all things God may be glorified through Jesus Christ, to whom belong the glory and the dominion forever and ever. Amen.* I PETER 4.10-11

SUGGESTION SIX: Why should you feel intimidated at defending the faith? As a Christian, you know the truth, and non-Christians not only do not know the truth, but aren't even certain if it exists! The Appendix: Five Biblical Principles I may Encounter Today!, brings together in a method you can easily understand and follow, a way of defending the faith that will prepare you for any non-Christian encounter.

NOTES

1 Hebrews 4.12
2 2 Timothy 3.17
3 2 Timothy 4.2
4 Matthew 5.13-16
5 Matthew 28.18-20
6 Matthew 6.10
7 Genesis 1.26-28; 9.1-4
8 Matthew 28.18-20
9 Matthew 6.10
10 See *Its Time to Un-Quo the Status: How to normalize the present abnormal culture of a non-Christian, upside-down world and turn it rightside up with Christian principles*, Buddy Hanson, (Hanson Group, 2006)

BUILDING A GOD-HONORING LIFEPLAN

In 1925 a young copy writer, John Caples wrote a newspaper ad for a correspondence music school that showed the creativity that would eventually land him in the copywriters Hall of Fame. The headline read, "They Laughed When I Sat Down at the Piano but When I Started to Play...!" As you might imagine, the ad copy goes on to describe how surprised and impressed his friends were, when they heard this correspondence school taught person play the piano. Unfortunately, if you or I were at a public forum we might well say, "They laughed when I said I'm going to present the Christian perspective on this issue."

In the midst of the collective non-Christian worldview in which we are living, and primarily as a result of poor teaching from American pulpits during the last century and a half, many people think pastors are only necessary to marry and bury people, and entertain the rest of their congregation for an hour on Sunday. But for any Christian who takes his profession of faith seriously to get up and speak on a cultural issue, the laughter by non-Christians would quickly turn to embarrassment as God's Word doesn't return to him "void." [1]

> *The problem with our culture is not that God's Word doesn't work, but that we are not working it.*

When attempting to figure out exactly why we are not "working" God's Word, it would be easy to come up with several lame excuses and rationalizations, but they would all ultimately come down to the uncomfortable conclusion that we really don't believe it! For the most part, we, like Adam and Eve, think our wisdom is superior to God's revealed wisdom, and that we are perfectly capable of living and governing ourselves on our own. Instead of being "obedience freaks," and conforming our worldview and lifestyle to His instructions, we act more like "control freaks," by attempting to control the outcome of everyday situations and events according to our ways and resources.

 Why do we live as though we have been issued two decision-making hats: a religious one and a real life one?

We know that God created a universe, and not a biverse. We also know that He created one set of ethics for us to use in all phases of our life, not two sets of ethics. However, too many of us live as though Moses came down Mt. Sinai with 20 Commandments, ten for our religious purposes, and ten for our real life purposes. Every Christian would say that such a proposition is ridiculous, so my question is, "Why do we insist on living as though life has two separate ethical realms?

In any other area of our life, when we are confronted with a problem, we do our best to figure out what works, then we begin doing whatever it is. In sports, we call that practice, which is why teams practice between games. It is also why actors practice between performances. It is why we rehearse speeches and presentations before giving them. However, when was the last time you practiced, or rehearsed what you would say to a typical objection from a non-Christian? Or when was the last time you practiced your Gospel presentation?

 Why are we so thorough in our preparation for everything else, but "wing it" when it comes to living-out our faith?

It's no mystery what the most common objections to Christianity are, (you're about to be reminded of 52 of them!) so why aren't we rehearsing our responses, just as we would the objections to a product or service that we might be selling? As Christians, we aren't "selling" the faith, but we should be "informing" our non-Christian neighbors about the options of living forever in Hell, or in Heaven.

Unless you are just beginning your career, you are also familiar with the typical situations which provide you a great opportunity to explain why you are, or are not taking part in certain business practices. As you well know, each Christian is to "be ready in season and out" to teach the Word. [2] This means that we should not be afraid of being called

- narrow-minded, or
- superstitious, or
- bigoted, or
- intolerant (this is undoubtedly the favorite expression of the politically-correct crowd, who are without a doubt the most intolerant people on the face of the earth!)

As Appendix One explains, it should be a very easy task to turn the tables on any criticism of Christianity that a non-Christian may use. Since they have to steal our ethics in order to make sense out of life, if we can just keep asking them to explain what they mean by whatever they are saying against us, they will sooner or later reveal that they are contradicting themselves by using Christian ethics to justify their non-Christian beliefs!

The first step in meeting any objection is to ask them to define their terms, then explain to them that they are stealing a Christian ethic and that you are certain that they didn't mean to do that and so you are asking them to provide another reason for their objection (and continue this process for as many "reasons" they present).

Next, have them define how they know what they know. For example, "How is it that you can be so sure that your objection is correct, when you admit that you don't believe in absolute truth?" Ultimately, your conversation with the non-Christian will demonstrate that all they have is their own opinions, which means that their ethics are based either upon majority opinion or upon the opinions of a tyrannical elite class. In either case, the ethics that are seen as acceptable today, can become obsolete tomorrow! This also means that they can neither prove Christianity wrong, nor prove that their belief system is correct!

Since many of the objections you encounter are familiar, ask yourself for one biblical reason why you are not rehearsing the answers to these objections and situations. You wouldn't expect the coaches of your favorite team to just show up on game day and coach the game on the fly. You expect, and demand that they put some serious thought into it before the game. And if you've ever seen a coach on the sidelines during the game look at his large sheet of plays for certain situations, you know that he and his staff have done their homework.

 Does Jesus not deserve homework on your part so that you can present Him in the best light instead of just coming up with something in the heat of the minute?

How to Build a LifePlan

I'm an optimistic person, and as such, I don't want to imply that just because a Christian is going about his or her Christian life "on the fly," it doesn't mean that they are intentionally meaning to disrespect Jesus. However, the bottom line is this is exactly what each of us does when we don't put Him first in our thoughts and actions. None of us would imagine that we could be successful in getting our personal computers to do some function that they were not created to do…no matter how well intentioned, or sincere we may be. As special creations of God, we are much more complex than a machine, but the truth remains that God not only created us, but also created rules by which we should live. Unlike computers, we'll still work and get results without living according to God's rules, but the results won't be pleasant. Think about it.

If we could make successful decisions without thinking about what God's rules say, then we would be smarter than God!

"Okay!" you say, "You've convinced me that I've been a complete dork. But how can God forgive me and what can I do to begin setting the record straight?" The good news is that you not only serve a God who has provided you with the correct rules for living, but a forgiving God who loves you. Repenting for our sins, however, doesn't merely mean that we are sorry for disrespecting God, but also that we, with His grace, will stop committing that sin. So, in repenting for living a life whereby we unintentionally have been disregarding God's rules for how we should live, we need to begin living according to them. This raises a couple of questions:

How do we do this? and

 Where do we start?

At first glance, creating a LifePlan could be an overwhelming concept, but it's really not that complex. Since many Christians appear to know more about sports than the Bible, let's use a football example. There are certain situations that happen in every game, regardless of whether it is a high school, college or professional. This is also true of life. Regardless of our vocation, regardless of where we live, regardless of how young or old we may be, there are certain situations that are common to all of us. And, how we react to them will go a long way in determining the amount of success and satisfaction we will attain.

Obviously, those who have anticipated these common and reoccurring situations will be best prepared to handle them. As you go about your daily duties, decision-making challenges may come to you at a fast and even furious pace. But do they come at you any faster than they do for a coach during a game? For example, which play would you call if your team had,

- Third down and three yards to go? Or,
- Third down and nine yards to go? Or,
- Second down and two yards to go at the goal line? Or,
- If there were two minutes to go before halftime and you were trying to score? Or,
- If there were four minutes to go in the game and you were trying to run out the clock? Or,
- If the other team had the ball how would you defend each of these situations?

Coaches are just as aware as you are that these situations will come up at one time or another in every game. With only about 30 seconds between each play, the coach doesn't have much time think about which is the right play to call, which is why you see them with a large play sheet we mentioned earlier that they are constantly looking at. This sheet has the various plays they have practiced during the week for these exact situations. Coaches know that key decisions shouldn't be made on the spur of the moment. They also know that their decisions will have a greater chance of success if they are practiced. Practice builds confidence and repetition hones your ability to execute the play correctly.

If it means something, you should practice it!

We all expect and demand that our coaches prepare our teams in this manner before each game, but why shouldn't we expect and demand the same effort from ourselves for the decisions we will face each day before we leave our home? Certainly our lifestyle is much more important than a game, so why don't we put forth the effort to make successful and God-honoring decisions?

How Can You Leave Home Each Day with the Confidence that You Will Make God-honoring Decisions?

Again, we take a lesson from football coaches. Many of them "script" the first 25 offensive plays of each game. These scripted plays include different positions on the field and perhaps three or four plays to choose from on each situation. Since time during the week has been spent on these plays, the players have confidence that they can correctly execute them, and the coach is relieved from having the pressure on him to decide which play to call next. He simply chooses from among the three or four plays they have practiced for each position on the field.

Is there any reason you can't "script" decisions for the most common decisions you will face during the upcoming week? Most of the decisions will be reoccurring ones, and depending upon your vocation, the unique decisions with which you will be faced will be pretty predictable.

The goal of *Making Your Daily READS* is to assist you in developing your script. You will notice that the Table of Contents groups all "audibles" under their appropriate topic, but that doesn't mean that you have to study them in that order. As you build your "script," you may want to select an item from each of the different READS for the first fifteen weeks. For example, by selecting one of the READS from each category, your first 15 weeks could look something like this:

WEEKS 1 – 9 – 16 – 23 – 40
WEEKS 2 – 10 – 17 – 24 – 41
WEEKS 3 – 11 – 18 – 25 – 42

This would mean that after your first 15 weeks, you, like your favorite team's football coach, would have three choices from each of the READS categories with which to oppose non-Christians and defend the faith. Following this process should take a lot of the pressure off you as you exit your home each day. You will also be more confident that you will be able to give your best effort in serving Jesus each day.

How to Approach the Daily READS

In football, there are a lot more situations to plan for and practice than there are in life. But think about how long it takes to practice a particular play in football…not very long, probably not longer than a minute. However, it might take a lot of practice time to correctly learn how to execute the play, but once you learn one of the READS, the coach, can simply blow his whistle, and shout out the play and the players will line up and run it. This same formula can be applied to *Making Your Daily READS*. First, give yourself enough time to build your answer and practice it, (which is why only one of the READS is presented each week), then as you get a couple of months under your belt, set aside a few minutes to review each one that you've learned. For example, if you've learned 10 of them, it shouldn't take you more than 10-15 minutes to mentally practice them.

If there are any football coaches, or any former players reading this, I'm certain you re-member having a portion of one of your weekly practices devoted to reviewing long yard-age and short yardage plays, plus a 2-minute and 4-minute drill, and other such plays. You can follow the same process with *Making Your Daily READS*. For example, you could set aside one Saturday a month to quickly review your READS so you can keep your answers sharp in your mind.

Any objection you encounter will fall under one of the five categories of READS. As you begin to make an effort to consistently live-out your faith by being both offensive (pro-active), and defensive (reactive), you will run into situations that you can include under one of the five categories of READS (indeed such situations may be discussed in either Volume II or Volume III). The important thing is being aware of who you are, what you have been called into Christ's Kingdom to do, and the knowledge that since the Holy Spirit has given you a new spiritual heart, only you and fellow Christians have the answers to all of life's essential questions. As a "child of God,"[3] you have been "called according to His purpose,"[4] and you should be most careful that you "walk worthy" of your calling.[5]

Since the "earth is the Lord's[6] and He has "given it to man,"[7] and promised that we will "knock down the gates of Hell"[8] as we gradually "subdue and rule over the earth"[9] and will eventually deliver a deadly blow to Satan,[10] we can have confidence that one day Christians will successfully reach the goal line of redeeming the earth for God so that everyone is living according to God's ethics, instead of man's ethics.[11]

> *For the word of God is living and powerful, and sharper than any two-edged sword, piercing even to the division of soul and spirit, and of joints and marrow, and is a discerner of the thoughts and intents of the heart.* HEBREWS 4.12

May we all pray with King David to "Let the words of our mouth and the meditation of our heart be acceptable in God's sight."[12]

The Field of Life

The Field of Life illustration on the following page follows our football example by comparing what God commands and the Bible instructs us to do for Christ's Kingdom. If this were a perfect world, we would be perfectly conforming our thoughts, words and actions to God's Word.[13] However, each of us is living proof that the world is far from perfect, still our goal is to do the best we can to conform ourselves, our family, neighbors and community to live according to God's laws instead of to the laws we invent. While we are fulfilling our duty Jesus promises that He will remain at the right hand of God the Father, where He will intercede for us and rule and overrule all that is happening on the earth, then, once we've completed our task of bringing about God's will on earth as it is in heaven, He will make His glorious return in judgment.[14] At that time Jesus will turn His Messianic Kingdom over to His Father and we will all rejoice and worship Him through-out eternity in Heaven.

THE FIELD OF LIFE

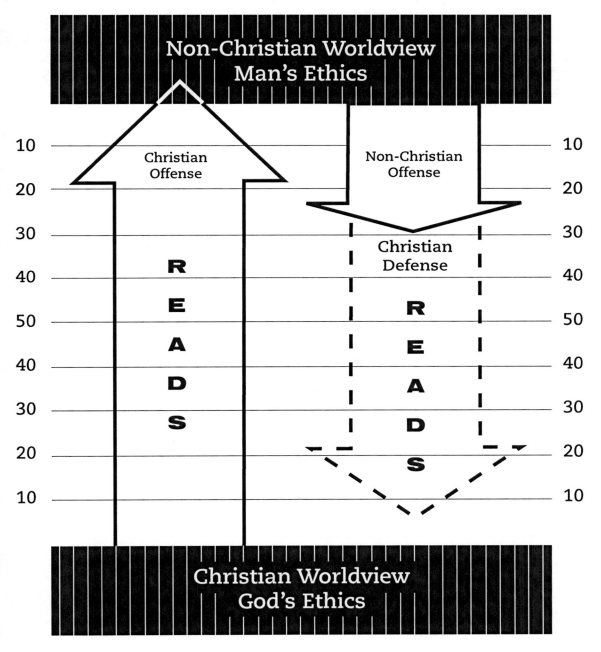

This is why the Christian Offense arrow is shown entering the Non-Christian's end zone. Conversely, the Non-Christian Offense arrow should be stopped deep in their own territory as long as we are faithful to live our life according to biblical truths. The dashed lines show a continuation of their progress toward achieving their hoped for complete non-Christian worldview. They will continue to succeed toward their goal only as long as we remain disobedient. History shows that disobedient nations are destroyed with their surviving citizens being cast into captivity. But, regardless of how much progress the non-Christians make in pursuit of their goal, they won't be able to ultimately succeed. God's eternally perfect plan for His creation will ultimately be implemented as He raises up obedient followers to carry out His will "on earth as it is in heaven." [15] In speaking of carrying out our defensive assignments, let's remind ourselves that there is no reason we should be caught off guard by the offensive strategies of non-Christians. Two of their most effective strategies is to say,

- "Life is made up of two realms: religious, and real life, and that each realm has a different set of ethics." And
- "All religions lead to heaven."

Your first response to these or to any other strategy or objection they proclaim is to ask them to "prove it from Scripture." Whether on Offense of Defense, our goal must be to turn the conversation to the Bible for support of any idea. This provides an objective and absolute reason for our beliefs. Without this all beliefs and their resulting ethics will be subjective and will be relative to either majority opinion, or the opinions of a tyrannical elite. If non-Christians refuse to base their discussion with us on this paradigm (which they will in order to be consistent to their ungodly worldview) politely break off the conversation. For example, after they make their statement, respond by stating something similar to the following:

Since the Christian worldview believes in a created universe by the triune God of the Bible, and the non-Christian worldview believes in a universe that "just is," with the earth and life coming about by "chance," we don't have any way of having a meaningful communication. The reason I say this is because, according to the Christian view, I can "account" for what I believe, and can show you absolute reasons (based upon God's Word) why my ethics are correct and yours are incorrect.

Your views, however, not only prevent you from proving my views incorrect, but also prevent you from proving to me that your belief is correct! (since your ungodly view believes in no absolutes) I have absolute ethics that have always been true, are true today and will be true tomorrow. You, on the other hand, have relative or existential ethics which, at best, are only true for a moment, but which by your own ungodly definition of them, are subject to change at the next moment.

I can also point to numerous civilizations throughout history that have sustained themselves as long as they based their civil government upon biblical ethics (Western civilization). You, on the other hand, can point to no civilization that has sustained itself based upon man's ideas of civil government (Eastern civilization). Of course, this is old news to you because your ethics place no value on the lessons learned from history, since you only believe in what is happening now, or as you like to put it, "in the moment."

So, since our ethical systems are so different, we have nothing upon which to base a meaningful conversation. However, if you should get to the point in your life where you want to achieve more than merely "seizing the day," and would like to know how to "seize the purpose of why you were placed on this earth," please get back to me and we'll talk.

This approach puts the ideological ball in their court to initiate any future conversation.

NOTES

1	Isaiah 55.11	7	Deuteronomy 3.20	12	Psalm 19.14
2	2 Timothy 4.2	8	Matthew 16.18	13	Romans 12.2
3	1 John 3.1	9	Genesis 1.26-28; 9.1-4;	14	1 Corinthians 15.25
4	Romans 8.28; 2 Timothy 1.9		Matthew 28.18-20	15	Matthew 6.10
5	Ephesians 4.1	10	Genesis 3.15		
6	Psalm 24.1	11	Psalm 119.105; Proverbs 30.5		

AUDIBLE "R"

ONE RELIGION IS AS GOOD AS ANOTHER

WEEK 1:   *It's not fair for non-Christian nations to be held accountable to God's Laws because they don't know what His Laws are!*

WEEK 2:   *Jesus is our personal Savior, but to say that He is also the Lord of our lives, and the King over civil rulers is going too far!*

WEEK 3:   *Why should we be so concerned about the "pluralistic mindset" that so many people have toward religion?*

WEEK 4:   *Christianity is "narrow and bigoted!"*

WEEK 5:   *I'm a Christian, but I'm not attempting to force my beliefs on others like those Christians on the radical right.*

WEEK 6:   *I've seen how Muslims persecute non-Muslims in their countries and I don't want a repeat of that in America should Christians control civil government. I don't want us to violate anyone's liberty of conscience!*

WEEK 7:   *Why is it a sin to send my children to public schools?*

WEEK 8:   *Should God's judicial case laws be enforced, or have they "expired?"*

SCOUTING REPORT
Fundamental Points That Can Be Used Successfully Against These "Defenses"

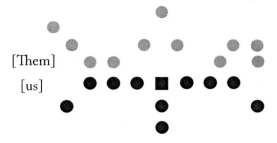

[Them]

[us]

Make Your Reads, and *Believe* What You Know

- It is critically important to determine which ethical standard our community's, state's, or nation's laws are based upon. Either our laws will be based upon an absolute set of ethics (The Bible, the antithesis of human opinion), [1] or a relative set of ethics (man's opinions, which means it can and will change with each change in civil government leaders), with everyone doing "what is right in his own eyes." [2]
- If we are not walking worthy of the vocation wherewith we are called, and are not living holy and obedient lives, we are saying with our actions, what we would never dream of saying with our words: That Jesus is our Savior, but not our Lord, and certainly not our King.
- For a Christian to live out of conformity to God's laws is blasphemy. Our calling is to conform the world to God's ways, not ourselves to the world's ways. [3] Scripture teaches, and history proves, that it is impossible for a civilization to sustain itself when its laws are based on a plurality of gods. The only ethical code (civil law code) that has a proven record of success throughout history is the biblical one.
- There is no mention in Scripture about a civil government being pluralistic in its religion. Indeed, the first commandment says we are to have "no other gods before us." [4] Therefore in submitting to civil rulers who are enforcing God's rules, we should also resist those who are enforcing man's rules. As long as civil rulers enforce God's rules, instead of making up rules (laws) of their own, citizens have no option but to obey them.
- The Creator God has revealed His inerrant Word and preserved it throughout the ages so that everyone can understand the proper way to live and interact with others. Our calling is to make His will known to our non-Christian neighbors through our words and our daily walk.
- Any curriculum that does not have the law of God as its centerpiece is not true education. God's Word is the foundation of how we should live and govern ourselves. It is our final authority over our conduct and beliefs. Since God's Word is true, this means that any educational system that is not based upon biblical principles is "false."

NOTES

1 2 Timothy 3.16-17; Acts 20.27; Deuteronomy 17.18-19; Romans 12.2; 2 Corinthians 10.5; Ecclesiastes 12.13-14

2 Judges 21.25
3 Romans 12.2
4 Exodus 20.3

WEEK 1
It's not fair for non-Christian nations to be held accountable to God's Laws because they don't know what His Laws are!

The point is not whether a community, or a state, or a nation has heard of a particular set of laws, but what standard their law-code is based upon. Either the law-code will be based upon an absolute set of ethics (The Bible), [1] or a relative set of ethics (man's opinions, which means it could change with each change in civil government leaders, with everyone doing "what is right in his own eyes.") [2] Moses teaches, "There shall be one standard for you; it shall be for the stranger as well as for the native, for I am the Lord your God." [3] God's perfect laws provide the best standard for anyone to live by, whether they are Christians or non-Christians. [4]

It should be remembered that John the Baptist didn't hesitate to apply God's law to the non-Christian King Herod (an Idumean) concerning his adulterous affair with his brother's wife. [5] Other Scriptural instances of non-Christian nations being held accountable to God's Law are:

* Sodom and Gomorrah, GENESIS 19

* Moses' instructions to the Israelites before going into the Promised Land,
LEVITICUS 18.24-30; DEUTERONOMY 4.6-8

* The Messiah's admonition to the kings of the earth, PSALM 2.10-12

* Isaiah's injunction that the earth will be judged when it doesn't live in accordance to God's laws, ISAIAH 24.5

* Jonah's message to the non-Christian nation of Nineveh, JONAH 1-4

* Paul's message on the righteousness of God's law for both Jew and Gentile, and ROMANS 1-3

* Jesus' proclamation that He did not come to "destroy the law," which emphasizes the continuity of the Old and New Testaments. MATTHEW 5.17-19

There is no getting around the truth that "righteousness exalts a nation." [6] Getting back to the question of "fairness," we must remember that since God's Law has been written on mankind's hearts [7] there is no excuse for anyone to claim, "I didn't know about God's Law!"

NOTES
1 2 Timothy 3.16-17; Acts 20.27; Deuteronomy 17.18-19; Romans 12.2; 2 Corinthians 10.5; Ecclesiastes 12.13-14
2 Judges 21.25
3 Leviticus 24.22; Exodus 12.49f
4 Deuteronomy 1.16; 24.16; 27.19
5 Mark 6.18; Exodus 20.14
6 Proverbs 14.34
7 Romans 2.12-16

IN YOUR OWN WORDS

Casting down arguments and every high thing that exalts itself against the knowledge of God, bringing every thought into captivity to the obedience of Christ.   2 CORINTHIANS 10.5

KeyPoints

_____

_____

_____

_____

_____

_____

_____

_____

_____

A Model for "Thawing the ICE" of a Non-Christian's Heart

Issue summarized
   Q. "What do you mean by that?"
   Q. "If that is the case, then what do you say about …?"
   Q. Point out the KeyPoints you listed in the above space.

Clarify the religion* associated with it (*worldview/philosophy)
   Q. "Upon what authority do you base your opinion?" (= "Why should I believe you?")
   Q. "Are you willing to base your eternal destiny upon your view?"

Expose it for the self-contradicting foolishness that it is.
• Repeat his presuppositions so he can hear how foolish they are
• Since their objection is going to be based upon subjective reasons, relate your questions to objective biblical reasons.
• Contrast its ultimate consequences (a consistent record of failure throughout history) with the historic record of success of communities, states and nations who have followed Christian principles.
• Explain which self-governing sphere(s) should be handling the issue (Individual, Family, Church, State).
• Present a humble, yet bold presentation of the Gospel

WEEK 2
Jesus is our personal Savior, but to say that He is also the Lord of our life,
and the King over civil rulers is going too far!

If we are not walking worthy of the vocation wherewith we are called, and are not living holy and obedient lives, we are saying with our actions what we would never dream of saying with our words "Jesus is our Savior, but not our Lord, and certainly not our King." Jesus, however, is the entire package: Lord, Savior and King, and He refuses to be chopped up to suit our self-centered agendas. Christ's Kingship is brought out in God's covenants with Abraham [1] and David. [2] In His office as King he rules according to His Father's will. [3]

> *Christianity is all about surrendering control of our lives to Jesus and submitting*
> *to His lordship.*

We would do well to remember that He commands us to pray that "His Father's will (not our will) be done on earth as it is in heaven. [4] Any attitude that stops short of this total and complete submission must be repented of, because it is an indication that we are clinging to our "old man" instead of to our "new man." [5] After all, think how silly a person's logic sounds who proclaims that Jesus is his Savior, but not also his Lord, or King!

The serious problems facing our country are not caused so much by those outside the Christian camp, as by those within. We know God's will, and they do not; and we have an insight into God's wisdom via the Holy Spirit, and they do not.

As Jesus, Himself, teaches, "The servant who knew His will and did not act according to it, shall receive many lashes." [6] For our country's sake, for our community's sake, for our children's sake, for our sake, indeed for the Lord's sake, let us each do what we can, where we are, with what resources the Lord provides, to trust God's promises enough to live according to His eternal truths.

> *Thus says the LORD: "Let not the wise man glory in his wisdom, let not the*
> *mighty man glory in his might, nor let the rich man glory in his riches; but let*
> *him who glories glory in this, that he understands and knows Me, that I am*
> *the LORD, exercising loving kindness, judgment, and righteousness in the*
> *earth. For in these I delight," says the LORD.* JEREMIAH 9.23-24

NOTES

1 Genesis 12; 17
2 2 Samuel 7.8-17
3 Psalm 2.6; Isaiah 9.6-7; 11.1-9
4 Matthew 6.10
5 Colossians 3.9
6 Luke 12.47-48

IN YOUR OWN WORDS

Casting down arguments and every high thing that exalts itself against the knowledge of God, bringing every thought into captivity to the obedience of Christ.　　　　　　　　　　　　　　　　　　　　2 CORINTHIANS 10.5

KeyPoints

_____

_____

_____

_____

_____

_____

_____

_____

_____

_____

A Model for "Thawing the ICE" of a Non-Christian's Heart

Issue summarized
    Q. "What do you mean by that?"
    Q. "If that is the case, then what do you say about …?"
    Q. Point out the KeyPoints you listed in the above space.

Clarify the religion* associated with it (*worldview/philosophy)
    Q. "Upon what authority do you base your opinion?" (= "Why should I believe you?")
    Q. "Are you willing to base your eternal destiny upon your view?"

Expose it for the self-contradicting foolishness that it is.
- Repeat his presuppositions so he can hear how foolish they are
- Since their objection is going to be based upon subjective reasons, relate your questions to objective biblical reasons.
- Contrast its ultimate consequences (a consistent record of failure throughout history) with the historic record of success of communities, states and nations who have followed Christian principles.
- Explain which self-governing sphere(s) should be handling the issue (Individual, Family, Church, State).
- Present a humble, yet bold presentation of the Gospel

WEEK 3
Why should we be so concerned about the "pluralistic mindset" that so many people have toward religion?

Pluralism sees all religions as being more or less the same. Obviously this attitude breaks the first commandment to "have no other gods before Me." (EXODUS 20.3) It is also important to understand that it is impossible for any society to be governed by more than one set of ethics. Either God's ethics will be accepted, or man's. Either man determines the civil laws, and their rewards and punishments, or God does. There can be no mixture. Sooner or later, we will either be ruled by God's absolute, unchanging, and personally liberating ethics or we will be ruled by man's ever-changing, tyrannical, and enslaving ethics.

The proponents of pluralism know this and have as their ultimate goal the abolition of Christianity and the installation of the State as "god." Part of their strategy is to object that we are being "narrow and bigoted" in our insistence on adhering to a set of absolute ethics. But whether they like to admit it or not, all people believe in absolutes: either they believe in God's absolute Word, or they absolutize the State, nature, the voice of the people, or something else. ...So, when God's Word is rejected something else is divinized.

Ultimately, we must decide whether the ideas under which we shall live are true or false. To compromise with the proponents of false ideas is to agree that our problem is not inside us (a sinful heart), but is outside us (bad environment, bad education). Such a position leads to dealing only with the symptoms of what ills society. The all-too-common results of a non-Christian cultural agenda are more government programs, higher taxes, and the continuation of the problems (because the cause, the sinful heart, has not been addressed).

The Nobel Prize-winning Irish poet, William Butler Yeats, once lamented, "The best lack all conviction, while the worst are full of passionate intensity." Let us determine to change this truism by refusing to go to Egypt for advice. Our priority must be to "walk in a manner worthy of God who calls us into His Kingdom and glory." It will only be when we live by Biblical principles that we will protect ourselves from being "carried away by varied and strange teachings."

Moses instructs civil rulers to live by God's Word, and to make their decisions conform to its principles.

> *Also it shall be, when he sits on the throne of his kingdom, that he shall write for himself a copy of this law in a book, from the one before the priests, the Levites. And it shall be with him, and he shall read it all the days of his life, that he may learn to fear the Lord his God and be careful to observe all the words of this law and these statutes, that his heart may not be lifted above his brethren, that he may not turn aside from the commandment to the right hand or to the left, and that he may prolong his days in his kingdom, he and his children in the midst of Israel.* DEUTERONOMY 17.18-20; ALSO 1 TIMOTHY 6.3-5

Casting down arguments and every high thing that exalts itself against the knowledge of God, bringing every thought into captivity to the obedience of Christ. 2 CORINTHIANS 10.5

KeyPoints

_____

_____

_____

_____

_____

_____

_____

_____

_____

A Model for "Thawing the ICE" of a Non-Christian's Heart

Issue summarized
   Q. "What do you mean by that?"
   Q. "If that is the case, then what do you say about …?"
   Q. Point out the KeyPoints you listed in the above space.

Clarify the religion* associated with it (*worldview/philosophy)
   Q. "Upon what authority do you base your opinion?" (= "Why should I believe you?")
   Q. "Are you willing to base your eternal destiny upon your view?"

Expose it for the self-contradicting foolishness that it is.
• Repeat his presuppositions so he can hear how foolish they are
• Since their objection is going to be based upon subjective reasons, relate your questions to objective biblical reasons.
• Contrast its ultimate consequences (a consistent record of failure throughout history) with the historic record of success of communities, states and nations who have followed Christian principles.
• Explain which self-governing sphere(s) should be handling the issue (Individual, Family, Church, State).
• Present a humble, yet bold presentation of the Gospel

WEEK 4
Christianity is "Narrow and Bigoted!"

Those making this objection are attempting to promote the false idea that there is no such thing as absolute ethics upon which to base our worldview and lifestyle. It could be said that they "absolutely believe that there is no such thing as 'absolute truth!'" However, the futility of their objection becomes apparent when we reply: "What is 'narrow,' and what is 'bigoted?'" According to their philosophy, they cannot define those absolutely. Therefore, there is no way for them to accuse Christians of being something for which they have no definition. (Indeed, if they are intellectually honest, they will have to admit that there is no word that they can absolutely define, which makes their entire attempt to communicate anything impossible and meaningless!) Consider the following examples:

- Would non-Christians object because Christians believe that parents, police officers, school teachers and others in positions of authority should be respected and honored (5th Commandment)? I think not.
- Would non-Christians object because Christians believe fellow humans should not be randomly killed (6th Commandment)? I think not.
- What about the exclusive Christian belief in marriage, instead of viewing women as sex objects (7th Commandment)? I think not.
- Would non-Christians object to the unique Christian belief that a person's property should not be stolen (or taxed) (Commandments 8-9-10)? Again, I think not.

I would hope these truths help explain that instead of limiting our personal freedom, Christianity widens it. In addition, for it to even be possible for non-Christians to tell us what they believe, they have to "borrow" some of our absolute principles (i.e., what is "good," and/or "bad" behavior).

> *There is no wisdom or understanding or counsel against the LORD.*
> PROVERBS 21.30

> *For whatever things were written before were written for our learning, that we through the patience and comfort of the Scriptures might have hope.*
> ROMANS 15.4

IN YOUR OWN WORDS

Casting down arguments and every high thing that exalts itself against the knowledge of God, bringing every thought into captivity to the obedience of Christ.　　　　　　　　　　　　　　　　　2 CORINTHIANS 10.5

KeyPoints

_____

_____

_____

_____

_____

_____

_____

_____

_____

A Model for "Thawing the ICE" of a Non-Christian's Heart

Issue summarized
　　Q. "What do you mean by that?"
　　Q. "If that is the case, then what do you say about …?"
　　Q. Point out the KeyPoints you listed in the above space.

Clarify the religion* associated with it (*worldview/philosophy)
　　Q. "Upon what authority do you base your opinion?" (= "Why should I believe you?")
　　Q. "Are you willing to base your eternal destiny upon your view?"

Expose it for the self-contradicting foolishness that it is.
- Repeat his presuppositions so he can hear how foolish they are
- Since their objection is going to be based upon subjective reasons, relate your questions to objective biblical reasons.
- Contrast its ultimate consequences (a consistent record of failure throughout history) with the historic record of success of communities, states and nations who have followed Christian principles.
- Explain which self-governing sphere(s) should be handling the issue (Individual, Family, Church, State).
- Present a humble, yet bold presentation of the Gospel

WEEK 5
I'm a Christian, but I'm not attempting to impose my beliefs on others like those Christians on the radical right.

Since non-Christians don't believe in the one and only true God of Scripture, they see all "gods" as being equally irrelevant. To their way of thinking, to seek any god's counsel, is to seek every god's counsel. Such thinking not only exhibits an illiteracy of Christianity, but an illiteracy of America's beginnings, which was not religious plurality, but the worship of the one true God of Scripture. The Christian response to their statement of not "imposing our beliefs" on others, should be, "Why not? Any Christian, aided by the Holy Spirit, has the ability to discern God's will from Scripture, plus we have been commanded to be "salt and light," and there is no way to obey that command without pointing out God's laws.

Often you will hear people preface this objection by saying, "I have nothing against Christians, or anyone else getting involved in politics, after all, I'm a Christian." They suppose that such a statement adds credibility to their indictment of Christian Civil Rulers who conform their legislative decisions to Biblical principals. What it really does, however, is demonstrate their misunderstanding of Scripture. Their god is little more than some undefined dispenser of salvation for the hereafter. The more undefined, and the less time they spend thinking about their god the better, because then they can imagine that they aren't accountable to act in any specific way toward him (or her, or it).

Obviously this type of thinking is completely unbiblical. The Creator God has revealed His inerrant Word and preserved it throughout the ages so that everyone can understand the proper way to live and interact with others. Our calling is to make His will known to our non-Christian neighbors through our words and our daily walk.

How long will you hesitate between two opinions? If the Lord is God, follow Him; but if Baal, follow him." But the people did not answer him a word.
I KINGS 18.21

The Gentiles shall see your righteousness, and all kings your glory. You shall be called by a new name, which the mouth of the LORD will name.
ISAIAH 62.2

No one can serve two masters; for either he will hate the one and love the other, or else he will be loyal to the one and despise the other. You cannot serve God and mammon.
MATTHEW 6.24

IN YOUR OWN WORDS

Casting down arguments and every high thing that exalts itself against the knowledge of God, bringing every thought into captivity to the obedience of Christ.   2 CORINTHIANS 10.5

KeyPoints

_____

_____

_____

_____

_____

_____

_____

_____

A Model for "Thawing the ICE" of a Non-Christian's Heart

Issue summarized
   Q. "What do you mean by that?"
   Q. "If that is the case, then what do you say about …?"
   Q. Point out the KeyPoints you listed in the above space.

Clarify the religion* associated with it (*worldview/philosophy)
   Q. "Upon what authority do you base your opinion?" (= "Why should I believe you?")
   Q. "Are you willing to base your eternal destiny upon your view?"

Expose it for the self-contradicting foolishness that it is.
*   Repeat his presuppositions so he can hear how foolish they are
*   Since their objection is going to be based upon subjective reasons, relate your questions to objective biblical reasons.
*   Contrast its ultimate consequences (a consistent record of failure throughout history) with the historic record of success of communities, states and nations who have followed Christian principles.
*   Explain which self-governing sphere(s) should be handling the issue (Individual, Family, Church, State).
*   Present a humble, yet bold presentation of the Gospel

I've seen how Muslims persecute non-Muslims in their countries and I don't want a repeat of that in America should Christians control civil government. I don't want us to violate anyone's liberty of conscience!

This objection may take the prize for containing the most inaccuracies. First, it presupposes that all religions are at bottom the same, therefore it is imagined that since non-Christians tyrannize the folks in their countries, so, too, would a Christian-influenced civil government. Those voicing this objection have not compared the teachings of the Bible to other religions. If they did they would know that Christianity promotes (indeed invents) personally-liberating bottom-up self government, instead of top-down central government tyranny. A brief comparison of Western civilization (which was founded on Biblical principles) with Eastern civilization (which was founded on false religions) should be enough to establish this point.

Second, in order for a Christian-influenced civil government to take place a majority of the citizens would have to be converted to Christ. Regeneration, not revolution would be the driving force behind it.

Third, being a non-Christian would not be prohibited. Everyone would have the freedom to live according to their personal beliefs and to worship whatever god they might imagine. Unlike the tyrannical practices other religions impose upon their citizens, a Christian-influenced civil government would allow for personal beliefs and the private practice of non-Christian religions. It should be seen, then, that under a Christian-influenced civil government no one's "liberty of conscience" would be violated.

> *When you come into the land which the LORD your God is giving you, you shall not learn to follow the abominations of those nations. There shall not be found among you anyone who makes his son or his daughter pass through the fire, or one who practices witchcraft, or a soothsayer, or one who interprets omens, or a sorcerer, or one who conjures spells, or a medium, or a spiritist, or one who calls up the dead. For all who do these things are an abomination to the LORD, and because of these abominations the LORD your God drives them out from before you.* DEUTERONOMY 18.9-12

> *And if it seems evil to you to serve the LORD, choose for yourselves this day whom you will serve, whether the gods which your fathers served that were on the other side of the River, or the gods of the Amorites, in whose land you dwell. But as for me and my house, we will serve the LORD.* JOSHUA 24.15

IN YOUR OWN WORDS

Casting down arguments and every high thing that exalts itself against the knowledge of God, bringing every thought into captivity to the obedience of Christ.   2 CORINTHIANS 10.5

KeyPoints

_____

_____

_____

_____

_____

_____

_____

_____

_____

A Model for "Thawing the ICE" of a Non-Christian's Heart

Issue summarized
  Q. "What do you mean by that?"
  Q. "If that is the case, then what do you say about ...?"
  Q. Point out the KeyPoints you listed in the above space.

Clarify the religion* associated with it (*worldview/philosophy)
  Q. "Upon what authority do you base your opinion?" (= "Why should I believe you?")
  Q. "Are you willing to base your eternal destiny upon your view?"

Expose it for the self-contradicting foolishness that it is.
•   Repeat his presuppositions so he can hear how foolish they are
•   Since their objection is going to be based upon subjective reasons, relate your questions to objective biblical reasons.
•   Contrast its ultimate consequences (a consistent record of failure throughout history) with the historic record of success of communities, states and nations who have followed Christian principles.
•   Explain which self-governing sphere(s) should be handling the issue (Individual, Family, Church, State).
•   Present a humble, yet bold presentation of the Gospel

WEEK 7
Why is it a sin to send my children to the public schools?

God's Word commands that parents bring up their children in the "nurture and admonition of the Lord." [1] Jeremiah tells us that we are "not to learn the ways of the non-Christians," [2] and the first commandment instructs us not to worship any other god than the triune God of Scripture. [3]

As creatures made in the image of God, how are we "imaging" Him by sending our children to schools who hate Him? Schools, by the way, which are willing to worship any god but Him?

Any curriculum that does not have the law of God as its centerpiece is not true education. God's Word presents the foundation of how we should live and govern ourselves. It is our final authority over our conduct and beliefs. Since God's Word is true, this means that any educational system that is not based upon biblical principles is "false." [4] So the contrast between Christian education and non-Christian education boils down to a contrast between a "true" and a "false" education. Or, put another way, a "true" and a "false" worldview. [5] For example, a true education must provide clear answers to the following questions:

- Who am I?
- Where did I come from?
- What is my purpose in life?
- Who is in control of the earth?
- Where am I going?

Christian teachers have as their primary responsibilities:

- Forming their students' minds to love and serve their Creator,
- Not just to teach a trade, but to cultivate the student's mind with biblical knowledge, and develop their reasoning for conversations with non-Christians, and last but not least to
- Pray for them and with them

Can it be imagined that public (government) school teachers approach their students with this mindset? We must not forget that Luke exclaims: "the child will be like his teacher!"[6] From this it should be abundantly clear that the public (government) schools are not an option. Neither we, nor our children are to be "unequally yoked together with non-Christians." [7] Christian parents must either home school their children or make certain they attend a Christian day school.

NOTES

1 Ephesians 6.4
2 Jeremiah 10.2

3 Exodus 20.3, 5
4 John 17.17; Psalm 119.151
5 Romans 12.2

6 Luke 6.40
7 2 Corinthians 6.14

IN YOUR OWN WORDS

Casting down arguments and every high thing that exalts itself against the knowledge of God, bringing every thought into captivity to the obedience of Christ.   2 CORINTHIANS 10.5

KeyPoints

_____

_____

_____

_____

_____

_____

_____

_____

A Model for "Thawing the ICE" of a Non-Christian's Heart

Issue summarized
  Q. "What do you mean by that?"
  Q. "If that is the case, then what do you say about …?"
  Q. Point out the KeyPoints you listed in the above space.

Clarify the religion* associated with it (*worldview/philosophy)
  Q. "Upon what authority do you base your opinion?" (= "Why should I believe you?")
  Q. "Are you willing to base your eternal destiny upon your view?"

Expose it for the self-contradicting foolishness that it is.
  • Repeat his presuppositions so he can hear how foolish they are
  • Since their objection is going to be based upon subjective reasons, relate your questions to objective biblical reasons.
  • Contrast its ultimate consequences (a consistent record of failure throughout history) with the historic record of success of communities, states and nations who have followed Christian principles.
  • Explain which self-governing sphere(s) should be handling the issue (Individual, Family, Church, State).
  • Present a humble, yet bold presentation of the Gospel

WEEK 8
Should God's judicial (case) laws still be enforced, or have they "expired?"

Should God's penal sanctions still apply to 21st century America? According to the most renowned biblical scholars of the 17th century, the answer is "Yes." In what is arguably the most trusted and relied upon summary of the Christian faith, *The Westminster Confession of Faith*, we read the phrase: "… sundry and judicial laws, which expired together with the state of that people." [1] Opponents of God's law say this means that the judicial (case) laws have "expired," instead of only the ceremonial laws (which Christ fulfilled during His earthly ministry). In order to come to a correct understanding of what the writers of the Confession mean, we must understand the difference between the words expired and abrogated. For example, section 19.3 of the Confession states that the "ceremonial laws are now abrogated," but section 19.4 states the "general equity" of the judicial law is "required" for all nations. Obviously, an "expired" law that requires "general equity" is a lot different than an "abrogated" law.

When section 20.1 states that Christians are now freed "from the yoke of the ceremonial law, to which the Jewish church was subjected," (i.e., bringing sacrifices) it is significant that the judicial law is not included in that "yoke."

God tells us that He does not "change" like we do, [2] so whatever is in the Bible still applies to us, unless it has been fulfilled (as is the case with the ceremonial laws). Consequently, the "general equity" of God's commands are universal and unchanging. Proof of this is seen in the case laws that are cited in the Confession in regards to Sabbath-breaking, false religion, idolatry, blasphemy, unlawful divorce, incest, fornication, bestiality, restitution for theft, etc. Also, there are numerous New Testament citations of the Old Testament case laws. [3]

The key to approaching biblical Case Laws is to look for the principles involved and see which of God's laws applies. For example, it was common for the Israelites to have flat roofs on their houses, which provided a good place to get some fresh air at night. Because it was a common practice to socialize on one's roof, each house was required to have a fence around the roof. Clearly, such a regulation would not apply to today's houses, but the principle of safety for our neighbor still applies. Hence, people have fences around their swimming pools and railings on stairs and porches.

- Do we really want to trust in man's ever-changing and imperfect opinions as to what penalties should be enacted upon criminals? Or do we want to trust in God's never-changing and perfect penalties as described and defined in His Case Laws?
- Which answer do you believe God would prefer?

NOTES
1 Westminster Confession of Faith, (1646, Westminster, England), section 19.4
2 Numbers 23.19
3 Matthew 18.15; Mark 10.19; Romans 12.20; 1 Corinthians 5.1; 9.9; 2 Corinthians 13.1;
   1 Timothy 5.18; Hebrews 2.2; 10.28; James 5.4; Matthew 15.4-5

IN YOUR OWN WORDS

Casting down arguments and every high thing that exalts itself against the knowledge of God, bringing every thought into captivity to the obedience of Christ.   2 CORINTHIANS 10.5

KeyPoints

_____

_____

_____

_____

_____

_____

_____

_____

A Model for "Thawing the ICE" of a Non-Christian's Heart

Issue summarized
  Q. "What do you mean by that?"
  Q. "If that is the case, then what do you say about …?"
  Q. Point out the KeyPoints you listed in the above space.

Clarify the religion* associated with it (*worldview/philosophy)
  Q. "Upon what authority do you base your opinion?" (= "Why should I believe you?")
  Q. "Are you willing to base your eternal destiny upon your view?"

Expose it for the self-contradicting foolishness that it is.
- Repeat his presuppositions so he can hear how foolish they are
- Since their objection is going to be based upon subjective reasons, relate your questions to objective biblical reasons.
- Contrast its ultimate consequences (a consistent record of failure throughout history) with the historic record of success of communities, states and nations who have followed Christian principles.
- Explain which self-governing sphere(s) should be handling the issue (Individual, Family, Church, State).
- Present a humble, yet bold presentation of the Gospel

AUDIBLE "E"

EDITING GOD'S WORD TO FIT OUR PRESUPPOSITIONS, INSTEAD OF ESTABLISHING ITS ETHICS IN OUR DAILY BEHAVIOR

SCOUTING REPORT

Fundamental Points That Can Be Used Successfully Against These "Defenses"

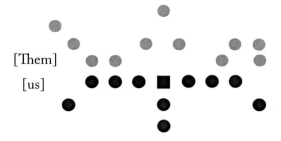

[Them]

[us]

Make Your Reads, and *Believe* What You Know

- For a non-Christian, or an ill-informed, or immature Christian, the concept of a sovereign, Creator God, controlling day-to-day activities is very demeaning. According to their worldview such a concept is unacceptable, since they see themselves as being "sovereign." The idea of an unchanging set of absolute values is completely unthinkable. Therefore they approach decision-making and policy-setting with a pragmatic, utilitarian mindset, where finding common ground is the goal and reaching an acceptable compromise is the modus operandi. For them, God is culturally irrelevant, and it is they who are the voice of reason.
- A Christian-influenced civil government would not make it a crime to be a non-Christian in one's personal beliefs and private worship practices. The advantage a Christian-influenced civil government would have is that all policy decisions would be discussed within a biblical framework (the truth!). The present day judicial tyranny would also disappear as Christian judges would rule on the basis of the absolute words on the law books, and not upon their self-centered social agendas (the truth!).
- Since it is impossible to separate one's religion (ethics) from one's day-to-day decisions, shouldn't our concern be about "corrupting culture with righteousness," rather than letting non-Christians "corrupt culture by their unrighteous and sinful ethics?" Yes, "politics" is dirty, but so is business, law, education, sports and every other activity. It's part of the human condition known as sin. We've been called to be a leavening influence in our communities for holiness. We can't carry out our Calling by keeping God's wisdom inside our homes and Churches. We have no option but to interact with culture.
- Satan will not be driven back by an instantaneous supernatural act of God, but rather by the obedience of Christians to God's commands and a faithful accepting of God's promises. In other words, our Calling is to complete the defeat of Satan.
- Each of us is a "work in progress," and despite our best efforts we will from time-to-time stray from basing our decisions upon biblical principles. At those times we should welcome loving counsel from a brother or sister.
- Living in a "cause and effect" universe, instead of one in which "random" blessings and curses are doled out by God means that we can expect to improve culture once we conform our worldview and lifestyle to biblical principles.

How do we know that the Christian God is the true God?

There are two dynamics involved in this objection. Non-Christians think they are smarter than God (which is only natural, since they don't believe in God). To their way of viewing the world, any "god" that a person worships belongs strictly to a religious realm while their work has to do with the nitty-gritty, here-and-now real world. They approach decisions pragmatically and don't see how any advice from any "god" could be helpful, especially since there are many different religions, each with its own definition of God. "Which God do we turn to for advice?" they may ask. For a non-Christian, or an ill-informed, or immature Christian, these concerns are very logical. To such people, the concept of a sovereign, Creator God, controlling day-to-day activities is very demeaning.

According to their worldview the idea of a sovereign Creator God makes people sound like nothing more than pre-programmed robots. For them, the thought of living according to an unchanging set of absolute values is completely unthinkable. Therefore they approach decision-making and policy-setting with a pragmatic, utilitarian mindset, where finding common ground is the goal and reaching an acceptable compromise is the modus operandi. For them, God is culturally irrelevant. It is they who are the voice of reason. And, when faced with a controversial issue, they commission a poll to find out what the people think about it, and how they should address it.

The thought of taking a particular course of action because God revealed an absolute and unchanging answer in the Bible, is unfathomable for non-Christians. In their view, the idea of absolute principles of behavior is discriminating, judgmental and unfair. "The voice of the people," not the "voice of God" is their primary priority. This is why they don't think it is necessary to submit to God. On the contrary, they expect for God to submit to the State by keeping in His proper place, which is the private and religious part of a citizen's life. To the non-Christian State's way of thinking, it, not God, is the true determiner and dispenser of "rights," and "rewards."

> *Then God said, "Let Us make man in Our image, according to Our likeness; let them have dominion over the fish of the sea, over the birds of the air, and over the cattle, over all the earth and over every creeping thing that creeps on the earth." So God created man in His own image; in the image of God He created him; male and female He created them. Then God blessed them, and God said to them, "Be fruitful and multiply; fill the earth and subdue it; have dominion over the fish of the sea, over the birds of the air, and over every living thing that moves on the earth."* GENESIS 1.26-28

IN YOUR OWN WORDS

Casting down arguments and every high thing that exalts itself against the knowledge of God, bringing every thought into captivity to the obedience of Christ. 2 CORINTHIANS 10.5

KeyPoints

_____

_____

_____

_____

_____

_____

_____

_____

A Model for "Thawing the ICE" of a Non-Christian's Heart

Issue summarized
- Q. "What do you mean by that?"
- Q. "If that is the case, then what do you say about …?"
- Q. Point out the KeyPoints you listed in the above space.

Clarify the religion* associated with it (*worldview/philosophy)
- Q. "Upon what authority do you base your opinion?" (= "Why should I believe you?")
- Q. "Are you willing to base your eternal destiny upon your view?"

Expose it for the self-contradicting foolishness that it is.
- Repeat his presuppositions so he can hear how foolish they are
- Since their objection is going to be based upon subjective reasons, relate your questions to objective biblical reasons.
- Contrast its ultimate consequences (a consistent record of failure throughout history) with the historic record of success of communities, states and nations who have followed Christian principles.
- Explain which self-governing sphere(s) should be handling the issue (Individual, Family, Church, State).
- Present a humble, yet bold presentation of the Gospel

WEEK 10
Are you saying that anyone who doesn't believe exactly like Christians will be discriminated against?

This objection imagines that a civil government based upon biblical principles would require all citizens to think and believe in exactly the same manner, or else face serious consequences. Perhaps the simplest way to answer this is to think about what is happening in our current civil government which is influenced by non-Christian principles. There are liberal non-Christians and conservative non-Christians who, while they disagree over certain policy decisions, certainly don't persecute each other. For example, the Democrats don't attempt to enact legislation making it a crime to be a Republican.

In a similar, but better way, a Christian-influenced civil government would not make it a crime to be a non-Christian in one's personal beliefs and private worship practices. The advantage a Christian-influenced civil government would have is that all policy decisions would be discussed within a biblical framework. The present day judicial tyranny would also disappear as Christian judges would rule on the basis of the absolute words on the law books, and not upon their self-centered social agendas.

Civil government has nothing to do with ecclesiastical matters such as how to baptize, whether to serve grape juice or wine at communion services, or how often to have communion. So, just as there are a variety of Christian denominations today under our non-Christian-influenced civil government, so would there continue to be under a Christian-influenced civil government.

But the end of all things is at hand; therefore be serious and watchful in your prayers. And above all things have fervent love for one another, for "love will cover a multitude of sins." Be hospitable to one another without grumbling. As each one has received a gift, minister it to one another, as good stewards of the manifold grace of God. If anyone speaks, let him speak as the oracles of God. If anyone ministers, let him do it as with the ability which God supplies, that in all things God may be glorified through Jesus Christ, to whom belong the glory and the dominion forever and ever. Amen.   I PETER 4.7-11

Remind them to be subject to rulers and authorities, to obey, to be ready for every good work, to speak evil of no one, to be peaceable, gentle, showing all humility to all men. For we ourselves were also once foolish, disobedient, deceived, serving various lusts and pleasures, living in malice and envy, hateful and hating one another. But when the kindness and the love of God our Savior toward man appeared, not by works of righteousness which we have done, but according to His mercy He saved us, through the washing of regeneration and renewing of the Holy Spirit, whom He poured out on us abundantly through Jesus Christ our Savior, that having been justified by His grace we should become heirs according to the hope of eternal life.   TITUS 3.1-7

IN YOUR OWN WORDS

Casting down arguments and every high thing that exalts itself against the knowledge of God, bringing every thought into captivity to the obedience of Christ. 2 CORINTHIANS 10.5

KeyPoints

_____

_____

_____

_____

_____

_____

_____

_____

_____

A Model for "Thawing the ICE" of a Non-Christian's Heart

Issue summarized
  Q. "What do you mean by that?"
  Q. "If that is the case, then what do you say about ...?"
  Q. Point out the KeyPoints you listed in the above space.

Clarify the religion* associated with it (*worldview/philosophy)
  Q. "Upon what authority do you base your opinion?" (= "Why should I believe you?")
  Q. "Are you willing to base your eternal destiny upon your view?"

Expose it for the self-contradicting foolishness that it is.
* Repeat his presuppositions so he can hear how foolish they are
* Since their objection is going to be based upon subjective reasons, relate your questions to objective biblical reasons.
* Contrast its ultimate consequences (a consistent record of failure throughout history) with the historic record of success of communities, states and nations who have followed Christian principles.
* Explain which self-governing sphere(s) should be handling the issue (Individual, Family, Church, State).
* Present a humble, yet bold presentation of the Gospel

WEEK 11
Why bother trying to improve the world? Aren't we living in the "last days?"

Every generation has had a number of Christians who were certain that theirs was the "last generation." Proponents of Jesus' immanent return apparently overlook His statement: "But of that day and hour no one knows, not even the angels of heaven, but My Father only." [1]

While it may be fun to speculate about the "secret things" of God, the thoughts that we are commanded to focus on are "those things which are revealed." It is from Scripture, not speculation, that we receive God's directions for living. Jesus' Parable of the Minas [2] speaks to the importance of being diligent in our day-to-day service for Him. In the parable, a nobleman has received a call to go to another country to receive a kingdom and he gives each of ten servants a mina (several months pay) and tells them to "occupy till I return." (v.13) Jesus' meaning of "occupying" becomes clear at the conclusion of the parable when the nobleman returns and asks his servants what they have done with their mina.

One servant reports he has earned 10 minas, and the nobleman praised him and put him in charge of 10 cities (civil government!), another's mina earned five minas and he was placed in charge of five cities. One, however had retreated from his service to his master and could only return the one mina that had been given to him. The irate nobleman rebuked him saying, "Why then did you not put my money in the bank, that at my coming I might have collected it with interest?" (v.23) He then took the mina away from that lazy servant and gave it to the servant with the ten minas. (v.24)

The answer to "Why bother trying to improve the world?" is because upon Jesus' return His immediate question to us is going to be how faithful have we been to apply Biblical principles to our situations and circumstances. After all, a friend of the world is an enemy of God. [3] Even though we can expect to encounter some persecutions for taking an unflinching stand for Christ's Kingdom, as His obedient servants we should have no other motivation than to do what we can to bring about His Father's will "on earth as it is in heaven." [4] We have no choice but to do so.

The only way for us to correctly carry out our calling in Christ's Kingdom is to consistently study His inerrant revealed Word, so that we will know what He expects us to do. Remember, our primary focus should be on God's revelation, not upon someone's speculation about when Jesus will return. Consider the number of hours you spend on your vocation, compared to the number of hours you spend on your hobby. For anyone to spend more time on their hobby than they do on their vocation, would no doubt result in their not having a vocation. There are several intriguing topics upon which we can spend a limited amount of time as a "Christian hobby." In addition to attempting to determine when Jesus will return, one could attempt to explain how we have three Gods in one, or how we are completely accountable for our actions, yet God is in sovereign control of us, or how Jesus was fully God and fully man during His life upon the earth. However, to spend more than a small fraction of our Bible study on these subjective topics, and to neglect the numerous objective commands of Scripture is to do our Lord, Savior and King, Jesus Christ a great disservice.

NOTES
1 Matthew 24.36   2 Luke 19.12-27   3 James 4.4; 1 Corinthians 7.23   4 Matthew 6.10

IN YOUR OWN WORDS

Casting down arguments and every high thing that exalts itself against the knowledge of God, bringing every thought into captivity to the obedience of Christ. 2 CORINTHIANS 10.5

KeyPoints

_____

_____

_____

_____

_____

_____

_____

_____

_____

A Model for "Thawing the ICE" of a Non-Christian's Heart

Issue summarized
  Q. "What do you mean by that?"
  Q. "If that is the case, then what do you say about ...?"
  Q. Point out the KeyPoints you listed in the above space.

Clarify the religion* associated with it (*worldview/philosophy)
  Q. "Upon what authority do you base your opinion?" (= "Why should I believe you?")
  Q. "Are you willing to base your eternal destiny upon your view?"

Expose it for the self-contradicting foolishness that it is.
- Repeat his presuppositions so he can hear how foolish they are
- Since their objection is going to be based upon subjective reasons, relate your questions to objective biblical reasons.
- Contrast its ultimate consequences (a consistent record of failure throughout history) with the historic record of success of communities, states and nations who have followed Christian principles.
- Explain which self-governing sphere(s) should be handling the issue (Individual, Family, Church, State).
- Present a humble, yet bold presentation of the Gospel

WEEK 12
Doesn't the Bible teach that Jesus' kingdom "is not of this world?" John 18.36

Objectors try to use this statement by Christ to infer that His kingdom has nothing to do with this earth. Such erroneous grammatical gyrations fall short, because a closer look at Christ's statement reveals He is referring to the origin of His kingdom, not its governance. Those holding this mistaken position are overlooking Jesus' Parable of the Mustard Seed [1] that teaches that the growth of His earthly Kingdom will spread throughout the entire world. Clearly, Christ's kingdom is in this world, not in heaven because once He returns in judgment He will send each person either to heaven or hell. [2] He will then deliver His Messianic Kingdom to God the Father and the Consummate Kingdom will then last throughout eternity. Besides, what possible meaning could Jesus' command to be "salt and light" to our non-Christian neighbors mean if the world is so unimportant?! [3]

None are more bold in censuring than those who least understand the things they censure. Therefore, we can expect to be roundly criticized by living out our faith.

- If we do any good works of charity we will be accused of being a hypocrite and that we are doing them solely to bring attention to ourselves.
- If we do our work away from the spotlight, we will be accused of being covetous, and having no good works.
- If we are pleasant, we will be censured as being vain, and
- If we are serious, we will be said to be melancholy.

We should all remember that in our sinful and imperfect condition we will not be able to be "friends" with non-Christians. After all, Jesus was perfect. He miraculously healed non-Christians of sicknesses and performed numerous miracles, yet they killed Him.

Fortunately, the only critique of our behavior that counts will be from Jesus on Judgment Day and we can be confident that no matter what is said about us on the earth, if we are striving to consistently conform our behavior to His Word, we will be complimented by Him then.

NOTES
1 Matthew 13.31-33; Ezekiel 17.23
2 Revelation 11.15
3 Matthew 5.13-16

IN YOUR OWN WORDS

Casting down arguments and every high thing that exalts itself against the knowledge of God, bringing every thought into captivity to the obedience of Christ.   2 CORINTHIANS 10.5

KeyPoints

_____

_____

_____

_____

_____

_____

_____

_____

_____

A Model for "Thawing the ICE" of a Non-Christian's Heart

Issue summarized
   Q. "What do you mean by that?"
   Q. "If that is the case, then what do you say about …?"
   Q. Point out the KeyPoints you listed in the above space.

Clarify the religion* associated with it (*worldview/philosophy)
   Q. "Upon what authority do you base your opinion?" (= "Why should I believe you?")
   Q. "Are you willing to base your eternal destiny upon your view?"

Expose it for the self-contradicting foolishness that it is.
*   Repeat his presuppositions so he can hear how foolish they are
*   Since their objection is going to be based upon subjective reasons, relate your questions to objective biblical reasons.
*   Contrast its ultimate consequences (a consistent record of failure throughout history) with the historic record of success of communities, states and nations who have followed Christian principles.
*   Explain which self-governing sphere(s) should be handling the issue (Individual, Family, Church, State).
*   Present a humble, yet bold presentation of the Gospel

As a preacher, I should not teach about cultural issues.

Our response to this all-too-common objection should be, "That's very interesting. Could you show me a Scriptural basis for your statement?" The objector certainly won't find it in any writings of the apostle Paul who told the elders at Ephesus, "I have not shunned to declare to you the whole counsel of God." The Bible presents perfect wisdom for how we should live. This includes principles to apply in our homes, churches, workplaces as well as in civil government.

Some objectors may refer to the person who asked Jesus to settle a matter of how to divide an inheritance with his brother, Jesus answered, "Who has made Me a judge or an arbiter over you?" [1] These brothers ask, "Doesn't this prove that pastors should only preach God's Word and not concern themselves with social or cultural issues?" Our response should be: "Are not commandments 5-10 about social and cultural issues? Are you suggesting that pastors be silent about stealing, murder, coveting, lying, etc.?" We should also point out that in making this reply Jesus was merely being careful to not usurp the God-appointed self-governing realm of the state.

One of the most watched portions of the local news is the weather forecasts. Even though we know they are not perfect, we tune in to see what the weather will be like tomorrow, so we can plan accordingly. But as important as weather forecasts are, think how much more important a "culture forecast" is for the congregation. Jesus rightly accused the Pharisees and Sadducees of knowing more about the weather, than how to subdue and rule over their culture.

> *Hypocrites! You know how to discern the face of the sky, but you cannot*
> *discern the signs of the times.* MATTHEW 16.3

Praise God that Jesus has not left us on our own to figure out how best to live and govern ourselves! Praise Him for that, but shame on us for not following His advice. In being faithful to preach the whole counsel of God, Pastors not only instruct their congregation in all facets of God's Word, they may also be preparing future Civil Rulers. Who knows whether there may be a future Mayor, Governor, or even President in one of their pews!

Will preaching the whole counsel of God and explaining how to incorporate biblical principles into all areas of one's life be a potential source of problems in some of the members? Very probably, but as the apostle Paul writes

> *Do I seek to please men? For if I still pleased men, I would not be a bondservant*
> *of Christ.* GALATIANS 1.10

Ultimately, the faithful pastor bravely serves His Lord, Savior and King for the same reason that every Christian does: It's where his "treasure" is, and he is determined to "seek first the Kingdom of God and His righteousness" in everything he says and does, [2] and because he "trusts in Him." [3]

NOTES

1 Luke 12.13-14   2 Matthew 6.21, 33   3 Jeremiah 17.5-8

IN YOUR OWN WORDS

Casting down arguments and every high thing that exalts itself against the knowledge of God, bringing every thought into captivity to the obedience of Christ.   2 CORINTHIANS 10.5

KeyPoints

_____

_____

_____

_____

_____

_____

_____

_____

_____

A Model for "Thawing the ICE" of a Non-Christian's Heart

Issue summarized
   Q. "What do you mean by that?"
   Q. "If that is the case, then what do you say about …?"
   Q. Point out the KeyPoints you listed in the above space.

Clarify the religion* associated with it (*worldview/philosophy)
   Q. "Upon what authority do you base your opinion?" (= "Why should I believe you?")
   Q. "Are you willing to base your eternal destiny upon your view?"

Expose it for the self-contradicting foolishness that it is.
•   Repeat his presuppositions so he can hear how foolish they are
•   Since their objection is going to be based upon subjective reasons, relate your questions to objective biblical reasons.
•   Contrast its ultimate consequences (a consistent record of failure throughout history) with the historic record of success of communities, states and nations who have followed Christian principles.
•   Explain which self-governing sphere(s) should be handling the issue (Individual, Family, Church, State).
•   Present a humble, yet bold presentation of the Gospel

WEEK 14
Why is it important that we live in a universe in which there are no random events?

From the Fall of Adam and Eve and continuing throughout Scripture God's Word is clear that He blesses us when we conform our lives to His Word and curses us when we conform our lives to the ways of non-Christians. [1] Living in a "cause and effect" universe, instead of one in which "random" blessings and curses are doled out by God means that we can expect to improve culture once we conform our worldview and lifestyle to biblical principles. In the first place we can observe all too clearly the success of the cultural agenda that is being implemented by non-Christians. Even though their ideas are wrong and will ultimately fail, they are achieving short-term success, because they are following an explicit plan to get them to where they think they want to go. The other reason for their "successes" is that for the most part, we aren't opposing them with an explicit plan of our own. (i.e., God's plan)

Another principle of Scripture is that for a temporary period of time, God will grant a society what it wants. Our society has spurned God's ways for man's ways and we are bearing the fruit of our wishes. Such an action toward a society by God is only a temporary measure, until it recognizes the error of its ways, repents and returns to living according to God's Word, or else continues in its disobedience until God destroys it. [2]

For those who view the world from man's eyes, the almost complete domination of American culture by non-Christians seems practically unassailable. "There's not a single influential cultural institution that they don't control," those in the "walk by sight" camp might say. However, those who walk (biblically) "by faith" [3] recognize that all of the successes by non-Christians have been accomplished without God, and since we have God in our corner, there is every reason to expect that once we begin living according to His will, instead of according to the will of non-Christians, we will begin taking ground for Christ's Kingdom.

> *Surely I have taught you statutes and judgments, just as the LORD my God commanded me, that you should act according to them in the land which you go to possess. Therefore be careful to observe them; for this is your wisdom and your understanding in the sight of the peoples who will hear all these statutes, and say, "Surely this great nation is a wise and understanding people." For what great nation is there that has God so near to it, as the LORD our God is to us, for whatever reason we may call upon Him?* DEUTERONOMY 4.5-7

NOTES

1 Leviticus 26; Deuteronomy 28
2 References for this are too numerous; read any of the Old Testament prophets for specific examples
3 Romans 1.17

IN YOUR OWN WORDS

Casting down arguments and every high thing that exalts itself against the knowledge of God, bringing every thought into captivity to the obedience of Christ.   2 CORINTHIANS 10.5

KeyPoints

_____

_____

_____

_____

_____

_____

_____

_____

_____

A Model for "Thawing the ICE" of a Non-Christian's Heart

Issue summarized
   Q. "What do you mean by that?"
   Q. "If that is the case, then what do you say about …?"
   Q. Point out the KeyPoints you listed in the above space.

Clarify the religion* associated with it (*worldview/philosophy)
   Q. "Upon what authority do you base your opinion?" (= "Why should I believe you?")
   Q. "Are you willing to base your eternal destiny upon your view?"

Expose it for the self-contradicting foolishness that it is.
• Repeat his presuppositions so he can hear how foolish they are
• Since their objection is going to be based upon subjective reasons, relate your questions to objective biblical reasons.
• Contrast its ultimate consequences (a consistent record of failure throughout history) with the historic record of success of communities, states and nations who have followed Christian principles.
• Explain which self-governing sphere(s) should be handling the issue (Individual, Family, Church, State).
• Present a humble, yet bold presentation of the Gospel

WEEK 15
Why is it wrong for me to form alliances and partnerships with non-Christians?

Paul's main point in his second letter to the Corinthians [1] is to not take part in false worship services and to not marry non-Christians. When a person deviates from God's explicit instructions on how He prefers to be worshipped, he should be aware that he is practicing a form of idolatry. Similarly, to date, court and/or marry a non-Christian is to ask for trouble, since they hate God. [2] Only the Holy Spirit can save an elect person by giving them a new heart, so there is no way we can hope to "save" a non-Christian, through any efforts or relationship on our part, regardless how sincere we might be, if that person is not one of God's elect.

When Paul asks, "What fellowship has righteousness with unrighteousness?" he is referring to the ultimate difference in how Christians and non-Christians view the world. The non-Christian looks to man as the ultimate authority of ethics and meaning, while Christians look to the triune God of Scripture as providing ultimate meaning. Even though Christians and non-Christians will agree on certain issues, the absence of a belief in absolute truth will prevent non-Christians from having anything meaningful in common with us (i.e., doctrine, fellowship, prayer). [3]

Paul concludes by contrasting the truth that Christians are children of "light," [4] while non-Christians are children of "darkness." [5] Indeed, it is our duty to "turn non-Christians from darkness to light." [6]

All of this is not to imply that we are to have nothing to do with non-Christians. Certainly we are called to present the gospel to them, but beyond that, our personal and business relationships should be confined to fellow Christians, with whom we should find agreement on how we should live, govern ourselves and carry out our vocations. Otherwise, it will be just a matter of time until our two ethical systems will come into conflict.

> *Do not be unequally yoked together with unbelievers. For what fellowship has righteousness with lawlessness? And what communion has light with darkness?* LEVITICUS 19.18; 2 CORINTHIANS 6.14

NOTES
1 2 Corinthians 6.14
2 Micah 3.2; Matthew 6.24; John 15.19
3 Acts 2.42; 1 Corinthians 1.9; 10.16
4 Luke 16.8; 1 Thessalonians 5.5
5 Colossians 1.13; 1 Peter 2.9
6 Acts 26.18; Romans 13.12; Ephesians 5.8-9, 11

IN YOUR OWN WORDS

Casting down arguments and every high thing that exalts itself against the knowledge of God, bringing every thought into captivity to the obedience of Christ. 2 CORINTHIANS 10.5

KeyPoints

_____

_____

_____

_____

_____

_____

_____

_____

A Model for "Thawing the ICE" of a Non-Christian's Heart

Issue summarized
   Q. "What do you mean by that?"
   Q. "If that is the case, then what do you say about …?"
   Q. Point out the KeyPoints you listed in the above space.

Clarify the religion* associated with it (*worldview/philosophy)
   Q. "Upon what authority do you base your opinion?" (= "Why should I believe you?")
   Q. "Are you willing to base your eternal destiny upon your view?"

Expose it for the self-contradicting foolishness that it is.
*   Repeat his presuppositions so he can hear how foolish they are
*   Since their objection is going to be based upon subjective reasons, relate your questions to objective biblical reasons.
*   Contrast its ultimate consequences (a consistent record of failure throughout history) with the historic record of success of communities, states and nations who have followed Christian principles.
*   Explain which self-governing sphere(s) should be handling the issue (Individual, Family, Church, State).
*   Present a humble, yet bold presentation of the Gospel

AUDIBLE "A"

APOLOGETICS:
DEFENDING THE FAITH AGAINST COMMON OBJECTIONS

SCOUTING REPORT

Fundamental Points That Can Be Used Successfully Against These "Defenses"

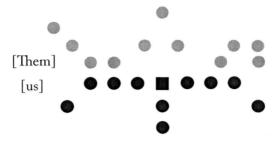

[Them]

[us]

Make Your Reads, and *Believe* What You Know

- Those who object to God allowing evil to exist should be asked to define "evil" behavior. In a world without God, terms such as "good" and "evil" are arbitrary and what is "good" for one person, may be thought to be "evil" by someone else, with neither party being able to prove their position.
- The phrase, "seeing is believing" is used by non-Christians in an attempt to discredit us from placing our faith in what the Bible says. However, by asking them how they became convinced that a person could only believe what he "sees," they will have to admit that some book or person convinced them of their imagined "truth" (which means that their beliefs are also based upon presuppositions and faith!).
- Atheists deny God because they don't want to be held accountable to God's moral standard. However, in denying their Creator, they are also denying themselves, because such a universe would be random and meaningless.
- Those who place "reason" over "faith" are building a false dichotomy. Without the absolute truths of Scripture, it would be impossible for anyone to be able to definitively prove anything!
- When non-Christians say, "All behavior is determined," and say that humans are simply "responding to circumstances in a conditioned manner," they must admit that to be consistent with their thinking, the civil government could not punish a robber if he grew up in a neighborhood that encouraged stealing because he would merely be acting according to the manner in which he was raised!
- Evolution is a theory that is not testable, and therefore is a philosophy, not a science.
- Those who say, "Miracles cannot happen, therefore Christianity, which is based upon miracles, is false," should be challenged to prove from their worldview how miracles are impossible.
- It is not uncommon for people to claim that their (false) religion can be tied to the Bible. After carefully listening to their reasons, we should ask the non-Christian to specifically explain what their religion teaches and how it is consistent with Scripture. In doing so we will find that ultimately they are attempting to avoid God's specific accountabilities for how they should live and govern themselves.

The Problem of Evil

OBJECTION: *Since God is all powerful and all good, there should be no evil happenings. Yet, since evil does exist, then God is either not powerful enough to prevent it, or He doesn't exist at all.*

Our first response to someone raising this objection should be to ask them to define evil. In a world without God, evil and good are simply arbitrary matters of opinion. By asking the objector to define his terms, perhaps he will see how silly his objection is.

On the other hand Christians can make sense of evil. It conforms to our basic presuppositions about reality, knowledge, and ethics. For instance, we know that God can and does use evil to accomplish His purposes. So, while we may not be able to explain a particular evil event, we know that,

> *... as the heavens are higher than the earth, so are My ways higher than your ways, and My thoughts than your thoughts.*   ISAIAH 55.9

RESPONSE: *How does your ethical standard enable you to define what is an evil action?*

Seeing Is Believing

OBJECTION: *We shouldn't believe anything that is not verified according to observation.*

By stating this, non-Christians think they are discrediting us for placing faith in God's Word. However, once we get the objector to talking about the superiority of their knowledge, they will admit that what they believe is based on someone's opinion, or information from a book. In other words, their knowledge is based upon the authority of another person, just as our knowledge is based on the authority of another Person.

RESPONSE: *Did you "see" the truth that tells that you can only know what you see, or did some book or some person convince you of that?*

IN YOUR OWN WORDS

Casting down arguments and every high thing that exalts itself against the knowledge of God, bringing every thought into captivity to the obedience of Christ. 2 CORINTHIANS 10.5

KeyPoints

_____

_____

_____

_____

_____

_____

_____

_____

_____

A Model for "Thawing the ICE" of a Non-Christian's Heart

Issue summarized
  Q. "What do you mean by that?"
  Q. "If that is the case, then what do you say about …?"
  Q. Point out the KeyPoints you listed in the above space.

Clarify the religion* associated with it (*worldview/philosophy)
  Q. "Upon what authority do you base your opinion?" (= "Why should I believe you?")
  Q. "Are you willing to base your eternal destiny upon your view?"

Expose it for the self-contradicting foolishness that it is.
*   Repeat his presuppositions so he can hear how foolish they are
*   Since their objection is going to be based upon subjective reasons, relate your questions to objective biblical reasons.
*   Contrast its ultimate consequences (a consistent record of failure throughout history) with the historic record of success of communities, states and nations who have followed Christian principles.
*   Explain which self-governing sphere(s) should be handling the issue (Individual, Family, Church, State).
*   Present a humble, yet bold presentation of the Gospel

WEEK 17
Atheism

OBJECTION: *Pleasure is all that counts.*

The reason a person claims he is an atheist is because he doesn't want to be held accountable to God's moral standard. [1] Atheists are not making their objections because they are smart, but because they are evil. What the atheist may not realize is that without God's absolute standard of behavior, he has no sure foundation for his actions.

A world without God means that events are the product of chance, not of purpose; they therefore are without a cause. So, for a person to deny God is ultimately to deny himself! What this means is that when a person attempts to "run from God," what he is really doing is "running from himself!" His complaints about particular people, events or circumstances amount to Shakespeare's "sound and fury signifying nothing." [2] The only way for him to find true meaning is to repent, [3] and turn his life over to Jesus.

RESPONSE: *If you think that the only things that can be true are those that can be proved by logic, explain how logic is possible without absolute truth. How does what you believe enable one person's logic to be "more logical" than the another person's logic? Besides, since you only believe in what you can see, feel, taste and touch, how can you believe in "logic," since it meets none of those criteria?!*

Naturalism – Faith vs. Reason

OBJECTION: *Religious faith would require us to sacrifice reason altogether and trust revelation!*

Your approach to this objection could be: "I'm very curious to know why you think there is a dichotomy in Scripture between faith and reason? How do you explain the prophet Isaiah's invitation to 'Come now and let us reason together?' [4] Or the fact that the apostle Paul reasoned with the Greeks from the Scriptures for three weeks, [5] Or, how Paul reasoned with Felix, [6] or when Paul told Festus, 'I am not mad … but speak the words of truth and reason.' Or why the apostle Peter advises all Christians to 'give a defense to everyone who asks for a reason.'" [7]

RESPONSE: *Without the absolute truths of Scripture, how would you or anyone else be able to prove anything?*

NOTES

1   Romans 1.18-25
2   "Macbeth," Act 5, Scene 5
3   Acts 17.30
4   Isaiah 1.18
5   Acts 17.2
6   Acts 24.25
7   1 Peter 3.15

IN YOUR OWN WORDS

Casting down arguments and every high thing that exalts itself against the knowledge of God, bringing every thought into captivity to the obedience of Christ.   2 CORINTHIANS 10.5

KeyPoints

_____

_____

_____

_____

_____

_____

_____

_____

_____

_____

A Model for "Thawing the ICE" of a Non-Christian's Heart

Issue summarized
   Q. "What do you mean by that?"
   Q. "If that is the case, then what do you say about …?"
   Q. Point out the KeyPoints you listed in the above space.

Clarify the religion* associated with it (*worldview/philosophy)
   Q. "Upon what authority do you base your opinion?" (= "Why should I believe you?")
   Q. "Are you willing to base your eternal destiny upon your view?"

Expose it for the self-contradicting foolishness that it is.
• Repeat his presuppositions so he can hear how foolish they are
• Since their objection is going to be based upon subjective reasons, relate your questions to objective biblical reasons.
• Contrast its ultimate consequences (a consistent record of failure throughout history) with the historic record of success of communities, states and nations who have followed Christian principles.
• Explain which self-governing sphere(s) should be handling the issue (Individual, Family, Church, State).
• Present a humble, yet bold presentation of the Gospel

WEEK 18
All Behavior Is Determined and Predictable

OBJECTION: *Humans are nothing more than robots responding to stimuli in a conditioned manner.*

If free will is an illusion and we only do what we have been conditioned to do, then how is a parent expected to discipline an unruly child and remain consistent with such a philosophy? Or, how could the civil government punish a robber if he grew up in a neighborhood that encouraged stealing?

RESPONSE: *If you really believe all behavior is determined and predictable, how do you prove it based upon your worldview?*

Evolution

OBJECTION: *At bottom, we're all animals (since we're "biological accidents"), and the human species just happens to be the most intelligent.*

The theory of Evolution is a way of looking at the world. Because of its many unknowns, it is a debate in the field of philosophy, not science.

RESPONSE: *Upon what scientific evidence is evolution based and upon what basis does evolution qualify as a science? There have never been any hard facts to back it up. The theory itself is not testable, and therefore does not qualify as science.*

Before I formed you in the womb I knew you; Before you were born I sanctified you; I ordained you a prophet to the nations." ...But the LORD said to me: "Do not say, 'I am a youth,' For you shall go to all to whom I send you, And whatever I command you, you shall speak. Do not be afraid of their faces, For I am with you to deliver you," says the LORD. JEREMIAH 1.5,7-8

For You formed my inward parts; You covered me in my mother's womb. I will praise You, for I am fearfully and wonderfully made; marvelous are Your works, and that my soul knows very well. My frame was not hidden from You, when I was made in secret, and skillfully wrought in the lowest parts of the earth. PSALM 139.13-15

IN YOUR OWN WORDS

Casting down arguments and every high thing that exalts itself against the knowledge of God, bringing every thought into captivity to the obedience of Christ.   2 CORINTHIANS 10.5

KeyPoints

_____

_____

_____

_____

_____

_____

_____

_____

_____

A Model for "Thawing the ICE" of a Non-Christian's Heart

Issue summarized
   Q. "What do you mean by that?"
   Q. "If that is the case, then what do you say about …?"
   Q. Point out the KeyPoints you listed in the above space.

Clarify the religion* associated with it (*worldview/philosophy)
   Q. "Upon what authority do you base your opinion?" (= "Why should I believe you?")
   Q. "Are you willing to base your eternal destiny upon your view?"

Expose it for the self-contradicting foolishness that it is.
*   Repeat his presuppositions so he can hear how foolish they are
*   Since their objection is going to be based upon subjective reasons, relate your questions to objective biblical reasons.
*   Contrast its ultimate consequences (a consistent record of failure throughout history) with the historic record of success of communities, states and nations who have followed Christian principles.
*   Explain which self-governing sphere(s) should be handling the issue (Individual, Family, Church, State).
*   Present a humble, yet bold presentation of the Gospel

WEEK 19
The Problem of Miracles

OBJECTION: *Miracles cannot occur, therefore Christianity is false.*

This is simply an effort to question what really separates Christians from non-Christians. It is to take for granted what the non-Christian needs to prove – that the Christian worldview is not true. In other words, the non-Christian is masquerading his personal prejudices for rational arguments and it simply won't work.

If the non-Christian's problem with miracles is, "Because there are laws of physics that don't allow for miracles," our reply could be: "That's why they call them miracles (they violate the laws of physics)."

After all, just because a child has never seen an elephant until it goes to a zoo, it doesn't mean that the elephant didn't exist until the child saw it. "We just know that miracles are impossible," insists the non-Christian. In response, we should have the non-Christian tell us how his worldview enables him to know that miracles are impossible.

RESPONSE: *How do you know for sure that miracles don't exist (just because you've never seen one)?*

False Religions

OBJECTION: *Our beliefs can be found on the pages of our religious books, just like you base your beliefs upon what you find in your Bible.*

Non-Christians who follow false gods should not be thought to be prime candidates for Christianity. In many cases they are not seeking after the Jehovah God, but rather a god. This is why they make up different religious theories that don't demand a lot of accountability from them. As in all of our other instances in defending the faith, we should listen carefully to what the non-Christian says he believes, and then ask pointed questions about any inconsistencies that he uncovers.

RESPONSE: *Why does this particular religion appeal to you and upon what standard is it based? For those who claim that their religion has a linkage with the Bible, we should use the Bible to refute their inconsistencies.*

IN YOUR OWN WORDS

Casting down arguments and every high thing that exalts itself against the knowledge of God, bringing every thought into captivity to the obedience of Christ. 2 CORINTHIANS 10.5

KeyPoints

_____

_____

_____

_____

_____

_____

_____

_____

_____

A Model for "Thawing the ICE" of a Non-Christian's Heart

Issue summarized
  Q. "What do you mean by that?"
  Q. "If that is the case, then what do you say about …?"
  Q. Point out the KeyPoints you listed in the above space.

Clarify the religion* associated with it (*worldview/philosophy)
  Q. "Upon what authority do you base your opinion?" (= "Why should I believe you?")
  Q. "Are you willing to base your eternal destiny upon your view?"

Expose it for the self-contradicting foolishness that it is.
* Repeat his presuppositions so he can hear how foolish they are
* Since their objection is going to be based upon subjective reasons, relate your questions to objective biblical reasons.
* Contrast its ultimate consequences (a consistent record of failure throughout history) with the historic record of success of communities, states and nations who have followed Christian principles.
* Explain which self-governing sphere(s) should be handling the issue (Individual, Family, Church, State).
* Present a humble, yet bold presentation of the Gospel

WEEK 20
The Fall of Mankind

OBJECTION: *The "Fall of Mankind" was only physical and did not permanently effect the mental aspect of our reasoning.*

There is a lot made about humans not being robots and being able to make our own decisions. This is true, as man has always had the ability to "choose." As a result of The Fall, however, our natural desires are always and only toward choosing evil. So, while we are "free to choose," our choices will always be marked by our sinful nature. In Jeremiah's words:

> *The heart is deceitful above all things, and desperately wicked; who can understand it?*   JEREMIAH 17.9

RESPONSE: *Our discussion with non-Christians should center on God's Word, because no matter how intelligent they may be, on their own they will never be able to come to the correct understanding about their relationship to God, or anything else. Once God performs supernatural heart surgery on us, the Holy Spirit enables us to overcome our sinful nature, and not only become motivated to live according to His will, but to study His Word and apply biblical principles to our lifestyle and incorporate them into our worldview.*

Are You Out of Your Mind?

OBJECTION: *Why are you a Christian? How can you reject your mind and believe in something without any evidence to support it?*

RESPONSE: *Let me ask you a question. You say that you're concerned that Christians are living more by faith than by facts. But did you know that of all religions, only Christianity requires that its believers follow a written, objective standard? Do you realize that non-Christian scholars have tried unsuccessfully for more than 2,000 years to disprove the claims of Scripture? They can't even find any instances of where it contradicts itself!*

The standard of truth by which Christians live is not based on mystical voices or eery visions, but straightforward, readable words that cover two thousand years of history. The words in these 66 books that have been found in eleven manuscripts, from several countries, dating from the 1st through the 6th centuries, all put forward the same message. So, I agree with your statement that "Blindly believing in something is a serious mistake." By the way, what is your standard of truth?

IN YOUR OWN WORDS

Casting down arguments and every high thing that exalts itself against the knowledge of God, bringing every thought into captivity to the obedience of Christ. 2 CORINTHIANS 10.5

KeyPoints

_____

_____

_____

_____

_____

_____

_____

_____

_____

A Model for "Thawing the ICE" of a Non-Christian's Heart

Issue summarized
   Q. "What do you mean by that?"
   Q. "If that is the case, then what do you say about …?"
   Q. Point out the KeyPoints you listed in the above space.

Clarify the religion* associated with it (*worldview/philosophy)
   Q. "Upon what authority do you base your opinion?" (= "Why should I believe you?")
   Q. "Are you willing to base your eternal destiny upon your view?"

Expose it for the self-contradicting foolishness that it is.
- Repeat his presuppositions so he can hear how foolish they are
- Since their objection is going to be based upon subjective reasons, relate your questions to objective biblical reasons.
- Contrast its ultimate consequences (a consistent record of failure throughout history) with the historic record of success of communities, states and nations who have followed Christian principles.
- Explain which self-governing sphere(s) should be handling the issue (Individual, Family, Church, State).
- Present a humble, yet bold presentation of the Gospel

WEEK 21
"Relative" or "Absolute" Truth

OBJECTION: *I'm a Christian, and I believe the Bible is God's Word, but I also believe that since it was translated by imperfect humans, it contains errors.*

Since we lost our ability to think and reason correctly by the consequences of Adam and Eve's sin, we need God's Word in order to know the correct way to live and govern ourselves. If God's Word were 99 percent true, how would we determine the "one percent" that was not true? To have only one percent of the Bible as untrue would therefore render the entirety of Scripture ineffective, because no one could know for certain what God's counsel was. King David and the Apostle John tell us:

> *The entirety of Your Word is truth, and everyone of Your righteous judgments endures forever.*   PSALM 119.160; JOHN 17.17

It is also worth noting that when David and Jesus say that "God's Word is true,"[1] they don't say, "Most of God's Word is true." The bottom line is that either God's Word is true, or it is not. God's Word, the Gospel, applies to much more than our initial acceptance, repentance, and conversion; it applies to every aspect of our worldview and lifestyle. Christians are urged to have their feet "shod with the preparation of the Gospel of peace." They must cherish "the hope of the Gospel [3] and live "in a manner worthy of the Gospel of Christ." [4] Christians are subject to the "royal law" [5] and are "within the law to Christ." [6]

Critics of the authenticity of the Bible neglect to mention that in the numerous manuscripts that have been found throughout the centuries, none have contradicted each other.

God's Word effects its purpose, [7] is self-fulfilling, [8] is settled in heaven, [9] endures forever, [10] is the Gospel [11] and should be proclaimed as "the power of God unto salvation to everyone who believes." [12]

We can all rest-in and trust-in the correct counsel of the divinely inspired Bible!

RESPONSE: *The beauty of Christianity is that it is based upon absolute and objective truth. False religions are founded upon mysticism and subjective ideas. Followers of false religions ultimately resort to subjective ethics, instead of basing their worldview and lifestyle on the objective ethics of the absolute principles of Christianity.*

NOTES

1 Psalm 119.160; John 17.17
2 Ephesians 6.15
3 Colossians 1.23
4 Philippians 1.27
5 James 2.8
6 1 Corinthians 9.21
7 Isaiah 55.10-12
8 Luke 1.37
9 Psalm 119.89
10 Isaiah 40.8
11 1 Peter 1.25
12 Romans 1.16

IN YOUR OWN WORDS

Casting down arguments and every high thing that exalts itself against the knowledge of God, bringing every thought into captivity to the obedience of Christ. 2 CORINTHIANS 10.5

KeyPoints

_____

_____

_____

_____

_____

_____

_____

_____

_____

A Model for "Thawing the ICE" of a Non-Christian's Heart

Issue summarized
  Q. "What do you mean by that?"
  Q. "If that is the case, then what do you say about …?"
  Q. Point out the KeyPoints you listed in the above space.

Clarify the religion* associated with it (*worldview/philosophy)
  Q. "Upon what authority do you base your opinion?" (= "Why should I believe you?")
  Q. "Are you willing to base your eternal destiny upon your view?"

Expose it for the self-contradicting foolishness that it is.
- Repeat his presuppositions so he can hear how foolish they are
- Since their objection is going to be based upon subjective reasons, relate your questions to objective biblical reasons.
- Contrast its ultimate consequences (a consistent record of failure throughout history) with the historic record of success of communities, states and nations who have followed Christian principles.
- Explain which self-governing sphere(s) should be handling the issue (Individual, Family, Church, State).
- Present a humble, yet bold presentation of the Gospel

WEEK 22
God is "Love"

OBJECTION: *How could your God be "loving" and send non-Christians to Hell?*
                          Matthew 7.23

Those voicing this objection should be asked to define "love." The Bible describes our situation in this manner: God created Adam and Eve with the ability to choose "good" or "evil." They chose evil and the result was that the entire human race would have its decision-making ability influenced by sinful desires. Since God's ethical standard requires perfect obedience, everyone will wind up in Hell, unless they repent,* turn to God and live according to His rules. However, in our sinful state, no one desires to do this, so God sends the Holy Spirit to change the hearts of His elect so we will recognize our sinful condition and turn to Him. Our escape from our eternal death sentence is therefore totally undeserved, and due to His mercy and grace. That sounds like love to me. As the Apostle John writes

> *In this is love, not that we loved God, but that He loved us and sent His Son*
> *to be the propitiation for our sins.*   1 JOHN 4.10

John also provides this explanation in his gospel:

> *For God did not send His Son into the world to condemn the world, but that*
> *the world through Him might be saved. He who believes in Him is not*
> *condemned; but he who does not believe is condemned already, because he*
> *has not believed in the name of the only begotten Son of God. And this is the*
> *condemnation, that the light has come into the world, and men loved darkness*
> *rather than light, because their deeds were evil. For everyone practicing evil*
> *hates the light and does not come to the light, lest his deeds should be exposed.*
> *But he who does the truth comes to the light, that his deeds may be clearly seen,*
> *that they have been done in God.*   JOHN 3.17-21

RESPONSE: *If everyone is going to heaven, regardless of how much they despise God's*
                will, then why did God make His Word known to us, even causing His Son
                to give His life to pay our sin debt?

* What does it mean to "repent?"

The Holy Spirit mercifully and graciously works in the sinner's heart, enabling him to realize that he is a helplessly lost sinner (2 Timothy 2.25; Zechariah 12.10; Acts 11.18, 20-21; Ezekiel 36.31; Isaiah 30.22). Upon seeing how ungodly his lifestyle is (Jeremiah 31.18-19) he gratefully begins to "put off" his "old man," and begins "putting on" his "new man," Colossians 3.9-10) by conforming his ways to God's Word (2 Corinthians 7.11; Acts 26.18; Ezekiel 14.6; 1 Kings 8.47-48; Psalm 119.6, 59, 128; Luke 1.6; 2 Kings 23.25).

IN YOUR OWN WORDS

Casting down arguments and every high thing that exalts itself against the knowledge of God, bringing every thought into captivity to the obedience of Christ.   2 CORINTHIANS 10.5

KeyPoints

_____

_____

_____

_____

_____

_____

_____

_____

_____

A Model for "Thawing the ICE" of a Non-Christian's Heart

Issue summarized
  Q. "What do you mean by that?"
  Q. "If that is the case, then what do you say about …?"
  Q. Point out the KeyPoints you listed in the above space.

Clarify the religion* associated with it (*worldview/philosophy)
  Q. "Upon what authority do you base your opinion?" (= "Why should I believe you?")
  Q. "Are you willing to base your eternal destiny upon your view?"

Expose it for the self-contradicting foolishness that it is.
  • Repeat his presuppositions so he can hear how foolish they are
  • Since their objection is going to be based upon subjective reasons, relate your questions to objective biblical reasons.
  • Contrast its ultimate consequences (a consistent record of failure throughout history) with the historic record of success of communities, states and nations who have followed Christian principles.
  • Explain which self-governing sphere(s) should be handling the issue (Individual, Family, Church, State).
  • Present a humble, yet bold presentation of the Gospel

AUDIBLE "D"

GOD IS DEAD WHEN IT COMES TO "REAL LIFE" ISSUES

SCOUTING REPORT

Fundamental Points That Can Be Used Successfully Against These "Defenses"

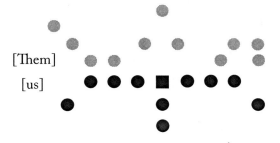

[Them]

[us]

Make Your Reads, and *Believe* What You Know

- A lack of respect of or trust-in the Word of God implies that our calling includes determining and controlling results instead of merely obeying God. We should never forget that we are creatures who have been called to serve God ... we are not mini-Creators who can control the outcome of events.
- Since God does not change, what He says in the Old Testament is still applicable unless He states somewhere in the New Testament that it has been annulled (i.e., that Jesus has fulfilled the Ceremonial laws).
- Those who say, "As a preacher, I should not teach about political issues," should be asked if they are not putting their wisdom (and imagined sovereignty) above God's wisdom and sovereignty.
- The expression "King of kings and Lord of lords" [1] means that Jesus is reigning over all kings and lords upon the earth, and that those who hold that title have been appointed by Jesus to bring forth His Father's will "on earth, as it is in heaven." [2]
- Jesus has given us the earth [3] to rule over [4] and promises that "the increase of the Christian government of it will not end." [5] In the meantime, Satan has no choice but "to flee" when we resist him. [6] None of these "rosy" consequences are happening today because far too many of us don't respect God's Word enough to obey it. Therefore, He is bringing curses upon us instead of blessings.
- All cultural questions are answered in terms of man's opinion or God's opinion. When it comes to making ethical decisions, our only options are man's wisdom or God's wisdom. For Christians, God is the sole determiner of truth, and for non-Christians, man is the sole determiner.

NOTES

1 1 Timothy 6.15; Revelation 17.14; 19.16
2 Romans 13.1; Matthew 6.10
3 Psalm 115.16

4 Genesis 1.26-28; Matthew 28.18-20
5 Isaiah 9.6-7
6 James 4.7

WEEK 23
Who are you to judge the actions of others? Don't you know that Christians shouldn't be judgmental? Matthew 7.1

Jesus' command to "judge not,"[1] and Paul's admonition "he that is spiritual is judged by no man,"[2] have led some to believe that Christians should not judge the actions of others. However, the context of Jesus' message shows that we must not judge others until we judge ourselves, while Paul is simply saying that a Christian has no business being judged by a non-Christian (a person who is not "spiritual").

Were this not the case it would be impossible to fulfill our duty to be "salt and light" in our communities by holding each other accountable to conform our actions to God's Word.[3] People would merely misquote "Judge not, that you be not judged" in an attempt to hide their bad behavior and prevent others from correcting them. Unfortunately for them, Jesus is not teaching that Christians are never to judge the actions of others. One only has to continue reading to verse six to see that Jesus calls some people "pigs" and "dogs," or to verse fifteen where he calls some people "wolves in sheep's clothing." Jesus' instructions in Matthew 18.15-17 on "judging a brother" also quickly dispel this myth. What Jesus is teaching here is that we must be careful that our standard of judgment conforms to the Bible, because the standard upon which we judge others is the one that will be used to judge us.

Since God's Word is perfect, His ethical standards regarding the way we should live, govern ourselves and relate to our neighbors are also perfect. Therefore, calling each other to repentance, combined with an attitude of care and concern conforms to our calling to be "salt and light" to those with whom we come in contact.[4] Each of us is a "work in progress," and despite our best efforts we will from time-to-time stray from basing our decisions upon biblical principles. At those times we should welcome loving counsel from a brother or sister. 800 years before the birth of Christ, the prophet Micah put it best:

> *He has shown you, O man, what is good; and what does the LORD require of you but to do justly, to love mercy, and to walk humbly with your God?*
>
> Micah 6.8

> *In all your ways acknowledge Him and He shall direct your paths.*
>
> Proverbs 3.6

> *By this is My Father glorified, that you bear much fruit, so you will be My disciples.*
>
> John 15.8

NOTES

1 Matthew 7.1
2 1 Corinthians 2.15

3 Matthew 7.3-5; 16.23; John 1.47; 6.70
4 Ephesians 4.15

Casting down arguments and every high thing that exalts itself against the knowledge of God, bringing every thought into captivity to the obedience of Christ. 2 CORINTHIANS 10.5

KeyPoints

_____

_____

_____

_____

_____

_____

_____

_____

_____

A Model for "Thawing the ICE" of a Non-Christian's Heart

Issue summarized
  Q. "What do you mean by that?"
  Q. "If that is the case, then what do you say about …?"
  Q. Point out the KeyPoints you listed in the above space.

Clarify the religion* associated with it (*worldview/philosophy)
  Q. "Upon what authority do you base your opinion?" (= "Why should I believe you?")
  Q. "Are you willing to base your eternal destiny upon your view?"

Expose it for the self-contradicting foolishness that it is.
• Repeat his presuppositions so he can hear how foolish they are
• Since their objection is going to be based upon subjective reasons, relate your questions to objective biblical reasons.
• Contrast its ultimate consequences (a consistent record of failure throughout history) with the historic record of success of communities, states and nations who have followed Christian principles.
• Explain which self-governing sphere(s) should be handling the issue (Individual, Family, Church, State).
• Present a humble, yet bold presentation of the Gospel

WEEK 24
What are some practical applications of having a biblical worldview? (Part One)

- **Trust In God's Sovereignty** – We should not let current circumstances blind us to the sure hope we have in God. No matter how bad a particular situation is, we must remember that God is in sovereign control of everything and will bring good out of it as long as we remain obedient. [1] Jesus has called us into His Kingdom and given us a message and a mission. The message is to be evangelistic with the gospel, and the mission is to be a discipler to individuals and even nations.

- **Live-out our faith** by connecting our Spiritual Dots (core biblical truths) to the ministry to which God has called us (i.e., our vocation) by living according to the principles of God's Kingdom, not those of man's kingdom. In doing this we will present a Christian alternative lifestyle for non-Christians to observe so they will know how God intends for us to live and govern ourselves. [2]

- Remind ourselves that *we don't control God's timetable* (our progress will probably be slow and gradual).

- **Think locally** – Thinking about the world's problems, or America's problems, or even our community's problems can be overwhelming. Where do we begin when there are so many worthwhile areas that demand immediate attention? One place that we know, unequivocally, where the Lord commands that we fulfill our leadership role is in our family. The biblical scenario has fathers carrying out and/or overseeing education in their homes, and families joining together in churches praying for each other's needs, enjoying each other's company, and being salt and light in their community. This type of lifestyle will solve local problems and provide the basis for solving the state, national and even international problems. We must begin with ourselves, our family, and our church. We should not expect to make a positive impact on the culture of our community until we have our "spiritual house" in order.

- **Look for opportunities to carry out our calling** to implement God's will on earth as it is in heaven. Offer solutions to cultural issues that attack their root cause, rather than dealing exclusively with "the fruit" that is falling from man's poisoned tree. Explain which of the four God-appointed self-governing spheres should deal with the various cultural issues: Individual, Family, Church and/or State. [3]

NOTES
1 Romans 8.28
2 Joshua 1.7-8
3 Matthew 6.10; Genesis 1.28; Matthew 28.18-20

IN YOUR OWN WORDS

Casting down arguments and every high thing that exalts itself against the knowledge of God, bringing every thought into captivity to the obedience of Christ. 2 CORINTHIANS 10.5

KeyPoints

_____

_____

_____

_____

_____

_____

_____

_____

_____

A Model for "Thawing the ICE" of a Non-Christian's Heart

Issue summarized
   Q. "What do you mean by that?"
   Q. "If that is the case, then what do you say about …?"
   Q. Point out the KeyPoints you listed in the above space.

Clarify the religion* associated with it (*worldview/philosophy)
   Q. "Upon what authority do you base your opinion?" (= "Why should I believe you?")
   Q. "Are you willing to base your eternal destiny upon your view?"

Expose it for the self-contradicting foolishness that it is.
   • Repeat his presuppositions so he can hear how foolish they are
   • Since their objection is going to be based upon subjective reasons, relate your questions to objective biblical reasons.
   • Contrast its ultimate consequences (a consistent record of failure throughout history) with the historic record of success of communities, states and nations who have followed Christian principles.
   • Explain which self-governing sphere(s) should be handling the issue (Individual, Family, Church, State).
   • Present a humble, yet bold presentation of the Gospel

WEEK 25
What are some practical applications of having a biblical worldview? (Part Two)

- **Lead By Example:** Our lifestyles are the only Bibles some people will see. Non-Christians will allow for our mistakes and shortcomings, because they know that no one is perfect, but they will quickly see through and reject any type of "Sunday-only" Christianity. As the only people who know how society "ought" to operate, we should not be hesitant to take leadership roles—in our church and in our vocation (*Westminster Confession of Faith*, XXV).

> *Therefore do not be partakers with them; for you were formerly darkness, but now you are light in the Lord; walk as children of light (for the fruit of the light consists in all goodness and righteousness and truth), learning what is pleasing to the Lord.* EPHESIANS 5.7-10

> *By this we know that we are in Him: the one who says he abides in Him ought himself to walk in the same manner as He walked.* 1 JOHN 2.5-6

Specific areas of our Christian worldview include:
  Apologetics: The basics of defending the faith.
  Economics: Capitalism vs. socialism
  Politics: The difference between Christian and conservative civil rulers.
  Social issues: Practical applications from the 2nd Table of the Law (commandments five through ten) and how the God-appointed self-governing spheres of the Individual, Family, Church and State cooperate in carrying out their specific responsibilities without usurping the responsibilities of the other spheres.
  History: The Reformation & American history plus the recognition that "history" is simply God's reactions to man's obedience or disobedience to His laws.

- **Teach the importance of the tithe**…this is how we finance the work of God's Kingdom.
- **Observe The Sabbath:** God has given us Sundays (The Lord's Day) to rest from our worldly endeavors and spend the day in private and public worship, and visitation, except for acts of necessity and mercy. It's a great opportunity to spend time with family and friends and to talk about, meditate on and pray over His Word. As our Creator, He knows our frame, which is why He gives us one day in seven to refrain from doing the kinds of things we do during the other six days. How far short many of us fall in observing the Christian Sabbath!

IN YOUR OWN WORDS

Casting down arguments and every high thing that exalts itself against the knowledge of God, bringing every thought into captivity to the obedience of Christ. 2 CORINTHIANS 10.5

KeyPoints

A Model for "Thawing the ICE" of a Non-Christian's Heart

Issue summarized
  Q. "What do you mean by that?"
  Q. "If that is the case, then what do you say about …?"
  Q. Point out the KeyPoints you listed in the above space.

Clarify the religion* associated with it (*worldview/philosophy)
  Q. "Upon what authority do you base your opinion?" (= "Why should I believe you?")
  Q. "Are you willing to base your eternal destiny upon your view?"

Expose it for the self-contradicting foolishness that it is.
• Repeat his presuppositions so he can hear how foolish they are
• Since their objection is going to be based upon subjective reasons, relate your questions to objective biblical reasons.
• Contrast its ultimate consequences (a consistent record of failure throughout history) with the historic record of success of communities, states and nations who have followed Christian principles.
• Explain which self-governing sphere(s) should be handling the issue (Individual, Family, Church, State).
• Present a humble, yet bold presentation of the Gospel

WHAT'S THE AUTHORITY BEHIND YOUR LIFESTYLE?

Man's Reasons for Not Living According To God's Will	God's Reasons For Living According To God's Will
1.	1. "He has delivered us from the power of darkness and conveyed us into the Kingdom of the son of His love, in whom we have redemption through His blood, the forgiveness of sins." COLOSSIANS 1.13
2.	2. After many of His disciples left, Jesus turned to Peter and asked, "Do you also want to go away?" Peter answered, "Lord, to whom shall we go? You have the words of eternal life." JOHN 6.68
3.	3. Paul tells us to be "steadfast, immovable, always abounding in the work of the Lord, knowing that our labor is not in vain in the Lord." 1 CORINTHIANS 15.58
4.	4. Paul adds, "And let us not grow weary while doing good, for in due season we shall reap if we do not lose heart." GALATIANS 6.9
5.	5. Abhor what is evil. Cling to what is good." ROMANS 12.9
6.	6. We should live "soberly, righteously and godly," being "zealous for good works." TITUS 2.12, 14
7.	7. "… that the name of our Lord Jesus Christ may be glorified in you…" 2 THESSALONIANS 1.12
8.	8. "That you may walk worthy of the Lord, fully pleasing Him, being fruitful in every good work and increasing in the knowledge of God; strengthened with all might, according to His glorious power, for all patience and longsuffering with joy." COLOSSIANS 1.10-11
9.	9. "Even so, every good tree bears good fruit, but a bad tree bears bad fruit." MATTHEW 7.7
10.	10. "Do you not know that the saints will judge the world?" 1 CORINTHIANS 6.2
11.	11. "On [My Word] I will build My church and the gates of Hades shall not prevail against it." MATTHEW 16.18; GENESIS 22.17

IN YOUR OWN WORDS

Casting down arguments and every high thing that exalts itself against the knowledge of God, bringing every thought into captivity to the obedience of Christ. 2 CORINTHIANS 10.5

KeyPoints

_____

_____

_____

_____

_____

_____

_____

_____

_____

A Model for "Thawing the ICE" of a Non-Christian's Heart

Issue summarized
   Q. "What do you mean by that?"
   Q. "If that is the case, then what do you say about ...?"
   Q. Point out the KeyPoints you listed in the above space.

Clarify the religion* associated with it (*worldview/philosophy)
   Q. "Upon what authority do you base your opinion?" (= "Why should I believe you?")
   Q. "Are you willing to base your eternal destiny upon your view?"

Expose it for the self-contradicting foolishness that it is.
   • Repeat his presuppositions so he can hear how foolish they are
   • Since their objection is going to be based upon subjective reasons, relate your questions to objective biblical reasons.
   • Contrast its ultimate consequences (a consistent record of failure throughout history) with the historic record of success of communities, states and nations who have followed Christian principles.
   • Explain which self-governing sphere(s) should be handling the issue (Individual, Family, Church, State).
   • Present a humble, yet bold presentation of the Gospel

WEEK 27
Where are we in fulfilling our calling to "subdue and rule over the earth?"

Where We Were *Before* The Messiah	Where We Are *Now*

1. There was worldwide
   a. slavery
   b. polygamy
   c. low social position of women and children
   d. political oppression and poverty of the masses
   e. brutal physical persecutions
   d. missionaries

2. The Gospel was mainly limited to the the physical nation of Israel and to a few proselytes

1. The growth of the church from 120 members in Jerusalem to millions throughout history.
2. The Gospel has spread throughout the world via:
   a. radio, TV, internet
   b. audio/video/DVDs
   c. print
   d. missionaries
   e. Bibles translated into many languages.
3. Commentaries and Bible study aids assist our growth in God's Word.
4. Early church councils which correctly applied Scripture against certain heresies.
5. Advances in medicine and health care.

Where We Want To Be

IMAGINED Hope

1. The establishment of an earthly kingdom that will provide:
   a. More material wealth
   b. Less trial/temptations
   c. Worldwide peace because Jesus' army will be superior to Satan's army.

BIBLICAL Hope

1. To continue to multiply and to subdue and rule over all creation. To bring glory and honor to God by giving the best effort that we are capable of to any task in which we are involved.
2. To train up our family in God's Word.
3. To evangelize/disciple our acquaintances as we assist in conforming the world to live according to biblical principles.
4. To live for God, not our selfish desires.

IN YOUR OWN WORDS

Casting down arguments and every high thing that exalts itself against the knowledge of God, bringing every thought into captivity to the obedience of Christ. 2 CORINTHIANS 10.5

KeyPoints

_____

_____

_____

_____

_____

_____

_____

_____

_____

A Model for "Thawing the ICE" of a Non-Christian's Heart

Issue summarized
   Q. "What do you mean by that?"
   Q. "If that is the case, then what do you say about …?"
   Q. Point out the KeyPoints you listed in the above space.

Clarify the religion* associated with it (*worldview/philosophy)
   Q. "Upon what authority do you base your opinion?" (= "Why should I believe you?")
   Q. "Are you willing to base your eternal destiny upon your view?"

Expose it for the self-contradicting foolishness that it is.
   • Repeat his presuppositions so he can hear how foolish they are
   • Since their objection is going to be based upon subjective reasons, relate your questions to objective biblical reasons.
   • Contrast its ultimate consequences (a consistent record of failure throughout history) with the historic record of success of communities, states and nations who have followed Christian principles.
   • Explain which self-governing sphere(s) should be handling the issue (Individual, Family, Church, State).
   • Present a humble, yet bold presentation of the Gospel

WEEK 28
You can't use biblical reasons for public policies without turning off the electorate. (Part One)

According to this objection, creatures, not the Creator, are imagined to be in control of God's creation. Such a gloomy portrait of God makes Him look small and ineffectual. Let's see what Scripture has to say.

- Does God's Word accomplish its purpose?

   For as the rain comes down, and the snow from heaven, and do not return there, but water the earth, and make it bring forth and bud, that it may give seed to the sower and bread to the eater, so shall My word be that goes forth from My mouth; it shall not return to Me void, but it shall accomplish what I please, and it shall prosper in the thing for which I sent it. ISAIAH 55.10-11

- Do non-Christians suppress truth in unrighteousness?

   I have written for him the great things of My law, but they were considered a strange thing. HOSEA 8.12

   For the wrath of God is revealed from heaven against all ungodliness and unrighteousness of men who suppress the truth in unrighteousness, because what may be known of God is manifest in them, for God has shown it to them. For since the creation of the world His invisible attributes are clearly seen, being understood by the things that are made, even His eternal power and Godhead, so that they are without excuse, because, although they knew God, they did not glorify Him as God, nor were thankful, but became futile in their thoughts, and their foolish hearts were darkened. Professing to be wise, they became fools, and changed the glory of the incorruptible God into an image made like corruptible man—and birds and four-footed animals and creeping things. ROMANS 1.18-23; ALSO 1 CORINTHIANS 1.18

   As it is written: "There is none righteous, no, not one; there is none who understands; there is none who seeks after God they have all turned aside; they have together become unprofitable; there is none who does good, no, not one."[a] "Their throat is an open tomb; with their tongues they have practiced deceit";[b] "The poison of asps is under their lips";[c] "Whose mouth is full of cursing and bitterness."[d] "Their feet are swift to shed blood; Destruction and misery are in their ways; and the way of peace they have not known."[e] "There is no fear of God before their eyes."[f] ROMANS 3.10-18

a. Psalms 14:1–3; 53:1–3; Ecclesiastes 7:20
b. Psalm 5:9
c. Psalm 140:3
d. Psalm 10:7
e. Isaiah 59:7, 8
f. Psalm 36:1

IN YOUR OWN WORDS

Casting down arguments and every high thing that exalts itself against the knowledge of God, bringing every thought into captivity to the obedience of Christ. 2 CORINTHIANS 10.5

KeyPoints

_____

_____

_____

_____

_____

_____

_____

_____

A Model for "Thawing the ICE" of a Non-Christian's Heart

Issue summarized
   Q. "What do you mean by that?"
   Q. "If that is the case, then what do you say about ...?"
   Q. Point out the KeyPoints you listed in the above space.

Clarify the religion* associated with it (*worldview/philosophy)
   Q. "Upon what authority do you base your opinion?" (= "Why should I believe you?")
   Q. "Are you willing to base your eternal destiny upon your view?"

Expose it for the self-contradicting foolishness that it is.
• Repeat his presuppositions so he can hear how foolish they are
• Since their objection is going to be based upon subjective reasons, relate your questions to objective biblical reasons.
• Contrast its ultimate consequences (a consistent record of failure throughout history) with the historic record of success of communities, states and nations who have followed Christian principles.
• Explain which self-governing sphere(s) should be handling the issue (Individual, Family, Church, State).
• Present a humble, yet bold presentation of the Gospel

WEEK 29
You can't use biblical reasons for public policies without turning off the electorate. (Part Two)

- Is God in sovereign control of His creation?

    For the Lord is our Judge, the Lord is our Lawgiver, the Lord is our King; He will save us. ISAIAH 33.22; ALSO ISAIAH 40.22-23

    Oh, let the peoples be glad and sing for joy! For You shall judge the people righteously, and govern the nations on earth.
    PSALM 67.4; ALSO JOHN 19.11

We don't need to be ashamed of our faith, and we don't need to disguise our Christianity with euphemisms, such as "Traditional Values," "Character Counts" or "Morals Matter." When we blithely throw around euphemisms, instead of saying what we mean, non-Christians, and/or moralistic Conservatives define them for us! The apostle Paul instructs

> *Do not be conformed to this world, but be transformed by the renewing of your mind, that you may prove what is that good and acceptable and perfect will of God.* ROMANS 12.2; ALSO ROMANS 15.4

To agree with this objection is to admit that God's Word is not truth,* for why else would we want to rely upon our words and ideas instead of His?

> *For the word of the Lord is right…* PSALM 33.4

> *Through Your precepts I get understanding; therefore I hate every false way. Your word is a lamp to my feet and a light to my path.* PSALM 119.104-105

> *Now all these things happened to them as examples, and they were written for our admonition, upon whom the ends of the ages have come.*
> 1 CORINTHIANS 10.11

> *Sanctify them by Your truth. Your word is truth.* JOHN 17.17

> *Therefore whoever hears these sayings of Mine, and does them, I will liken him to a wise man who built his house on the rock; and the rain descended, the floods came, and the winds blew and beat on that house; and it did not fall, for it was founded on the rock. But everyone who hears these sayings of Mine, and does not do them will be like a foolish man who built his house on the sand: and the rain descended, the floods came, and the winds blew and beat on that house; and it fell. And great was its fall.* MATTHEW 7.24-27; ALSO MATTHEW 15.9

IN YOUR OWN WORDS

Casting down arguments and every high thing that exalts itself against the knowledge of God, bringing every thought into captivity to the obedience of Christ. 2 CORINTHIANS 10.5

KeyPoints

_____

_____

_____

_____

_____

_____

_____

_____

_____

_____

A Model for "Thawing the ICE" of a Non-Christian's Heart

Issue summarized
  Q. "What do you mean by that?"
  Q. "If that is the case, then what do you say about ...?"
  Q. Point out the KeyPoints you listed in the above space.

Clarify the religion* associated with it (*worldview/philosophy)
  Q. "Upon what authority do you base your opinion?" (= "Why should I believe you?")
  Q. "Are you willing to base your eternal destiny upon your view?"

Expose it for the self-contradicting foolishness that it is.
• Repeat his presuppositions so he can hear how foolish they are
• Since their objection is going to be based upon subjective reasons, relate your questions to objective biblical reasons.
• Contrast its ultimate consequences (a consistent record of failure throughout history) with the historic record of success of communities, states and nations who have followed Christian principles.
• Explain which self-governing sphere(s) should be handling the issue (Individual, Family, Church, State).
• Present a humble, yet bold presentation of the Gospel

WEEK 30
Christians won't be able to restrain their religious views if they get elected to office.

Non-Christians have used this tactic very effectively to keep us out of the arena where social policy is affected. It's "the myth of neutrality." Christians are told, "You can be involved in social issues, but you cannot bring in your religious convictions. You must be neutral." The assumption being that those who are formulating public policy issues are also being neutral. But, of course, we know that no one is neutral. Each of us bring our ethical biases to every decision we make. The truth is that any worldview, whether Christian or non-Christian, reflects a person's religion. The issue, then, is not whether a person will restrain his or her religious views, because no one will. Rather, the question is "Upon what standard is a particular religion based?" In other words, what authority backs up a person's beliefs and gives them credibility? Statist socialism is all about power and influence. For the political party, it is about getting in office and staying in office. For the citizen, it's about losing personal liberty with each succeeding civil government program.

When America's first justice of the Supreme Court, John Jay, said: "Americans should select and prefer Christians as their rulers," he was emphasizing the fact that only Christians have been enabled to know the truth of God's Word, which among other things tells us how to govern ourselves. We must never forget that our goal is to do what we can to Christianize the inner man of our Christian brothers and sisters, while the goal of non-Christians is to Marxize the inner man of each of us!

By politely accepting the ideas and agenda of non-Christian legislators, we are conforming ourselves to their cultural pluralism, which immediately breaks God's first commandment to "have no other gods before Me." (Exodus 20.3)

The fourth president of the United States gave us this heartfelt counsel:

> *The belief in a God All Powerful wise and good, is so essential to the moral order of the world and to the happiness of man, that arguments which enforce it cannot be drawn from too many sources nor adapted with too much solicitude to the different characters and capacities impressed with it.*
>
> JAMES MADISON

IN YOUR OWN WORDS

Casting down arguments and every high thing that exalts itself against the knowledge of God, bringing every thought into captivity to the obedience of Christ. 2 CORINTHIANS 10.5

KeyPoints

_____

_____

_____

_____

_____

_____

_____

_____

_____

_____

A Model for "Thawing the ICE" of a Non-Christian's Heart

Issue summarized
  Q. "What do you mean by that?"
  Q. "If that is the case, then what do you say about …?"
  Q. Point out the KeyPoints you listed in the above space.

Clarify the religion* associated with it (*worldview/philosophy)
  Q. "Upon what authority do you base your opinion?" (= "Why should I believe you?")
  Q. "Are you willing to base your eternal destiny upon your view?"

Expose it for the self-contradicting foolishness that it is.
* Repeat his presuppositions so he can hear how foolish they are
* Since their objection is going to be based upon subjective reasons, relate your questions to objective biblical reasons.
* Contrast its ultimate consequences (a consistent record of failure throughout history) with the historic record of success of communities, states and nations who have followed Christian principles.
* Explain which self-governing sphere(s) should be handling the issue (Individual, Family, Church, State).
* Present a humble, yet bold presentation of the Gospel

Explain the significance of Christ being "King of kings and Lord of lords."

During His earthly ministry, Jesus perfectly fulfilled the offices of a prophet (teacher), priest (praying for us), and king (ruler and lord over the earth). In doing so, He provided models of behavior that we can follow to fill these three offices during our life. Most of us are "kings" over our households and perhaps a business, and some are called to fulfill this office as a civil ruler. In all cases, we are to be careful that in carrying out our duties, our behavior and decisions conform to biblical principles.

The expression "King of kings and Lord of lords" [1] means that Jesus is reigning over all kings and lords upon the earth, and that those who hold that title have been appointed by Jesus to bring forth His Father's will "on earth, as it is in heaven." [2] King Solomon proclaims:

> *Wisdom calls aloud outside; she raises her voice in the open squares. She cries out in the chief concourses, at the openings of the gates in the city she speaks her words: "How long, you simple ones, will you love simplicity? For scorners delight in their scorning, and fools hate knowledge. Turn at my rebuke; surely I will pour out my spirit on you; I will make my words known to you.*
>
> *Because I have called and you refused, I have stretched out my hand and no one regarded, because you disdained all my counsel, and would have none of my rebuke, I also will laugh at your calamity; I will mock when your terror comes, when your terror comes like a storm, and your destruction comes like a whirlwind, when distress and anguish come upon you.*
>
> *Then they will call on me, but I will not answer; they will seek me diligently, but they will not find me. Because they hated knowledge and did not choose the fear of the LORD, they would have none of my counsel and despised my every rebuke. Therefore they shall eat the fruit of their own way, and be filled to the full with their own fancies. For the turning away of the simple will slay them, and the complacency of fools will destroy them; but whoever listens to me will dwell safely, and will be secure, without fear of evil.* PROVERBS 1.20-33

The apostle Paul, in the beginning of his letter to Timothy declares:

> *Now to the King, eternal, immortal, invisible, to God who alone is wise, be honor and glory forever and ever. Amen.* 1 TIMOTHY 1.17

NOTES
1   1 Timothy 6.15; Revelation 17.14; 19.16
2   Romans 13.1; Matthew 6.10

IN YOUR OWN WORDS

Casting down arguments and every high thing that exalts itself against the knowledge of God, bringing every thought into captivity to the obedience of Christ.   2 CORINTHIANS 10.5

KeyPoints

_____

_____

_____

_____

_____

_____

_____

_____

_____

A Model for "Thawing the ICE" of a Non-Christian's Heart

Issue summarized
  Q. "What do you mean by that?"
  Q. "If that is the case, then what do you say about …?"
  Q. Point out the KeyPoints you listed in the above space.

Clarify the religion* associated with it (*worldview/philosophy)
  Q. "Upon what authority do you base your opinion?" (= "Why should I believe you?")
  Q. "Are you willing to base your eternal destiny upon your view?"

Expose it for the self-contradicting foolishness that it is.
• Repeat his presuppositions so he can hear how foolish they are
• Since their objection is going to be based upon subjective reasons, relate your questions to objective biblical reasons.
• Contrast its ultimate consequences (a consistent record of failure throughout history) with the historic record of success of communities, states and nations who have followed Christian principles.
• Explain which self-governing sphere(s) should be handling the issue (Individual, Family, Church, State).
• Present a humble, yet bold presentation of the Gospel

Why is it said that, a God-honoring, holy lifestyle doesn't just happen by osmosis as we gaze at our Bible on the coffee table?

Growing in God's grace and knowledge requires diligent effort as we "prepare our heart to seek the law of the LORD and to teach what we learn to others. [1] In contrast to the godly Ezra, King Rehoboam "did evil because he did not prepare his heart to seek the LORD." [2] This process of holiness includes several key factors:

1. Removing non-Christians viruses: We must clear from our worldview all of the non-Christian viruses that have crept in over the years. [3]

2. To avoid being unequally yoked: The only way we can hope to "observe and obey" God's rules [4] is to make certain that our circle of friends and associates are fellow Christians. [5] King Solomon counsels: "He who walks with wise men will be wise, but the companion of fools will be destroyed." [6]

3. Living by God's rules only: To paraphrase Martin Luther, we must live by Scripture alone, rather than by Scripture and tradition. Reminding ourselves of God's continuing blessings toward us and our merciful liberation from Satan's plantation will enable us to keep our focus on our service to our Lord, Savior and King, Jesus Christ. [7] Moses instructed the Israelites to "put a blue thread on the corners of their garments" so that when they noticed it they would be reminded of "all the commandments of the LORD and do them." [8] Our daily Quiet Time could provide an excellent opportunity to remind us to conform our daily decisions and actions to God's rules.

Isaiah's admonition to the Southern kingdom ring just as true for us as they did when spoken 2,700 years ago:

> *Seek the LORD while He may be found, call upon Him while He is near.*
> *Let the wicked forsake his way, and the unrighteous man his thoughts; let him*
> *return to the LORD, and He will have mercy on him, and to our God, for He*
> *will abundantly pardon.*   ISAIAH 55.6-7

A famous and well-loved verse of Scripture is found in verse eight of chapter six of Micah's prophecy: "He has shown you, O man, what is good, and what does the LORD require of you but to do justly, to love mercy, and to walk humbly with your God?" It may be surprising to some to find out that the context of this verse is serving our Lord from a sincere heart, instead of an insincere and hypocritical one. In verses six and seven Jehovah quotes the Northern kingdom's general attitude of serving Him as being: "LORD, we love You and want to serve You, so tell us what we need to do so we will know the best way to worship you. Should we bring burnt offerings, oil, even our firstborn child? Just tell us and we'll do it."

NOTES

1 Ezra 7.10
2 2 Chronicles 12.14
3 Leviticus 18.3-5

4 Deuteronomy 12.28,30,32; 4.2; 13.18; Joshua 1.7; Proverbs 30.6; Revelation 22.18-19
5 2 Corinthians 6.14

6 Proverbs 13.20
7 Psalm 119.45
8 Numbers 15.38-40

IN YOUR OWN WORDS

Casting down arguments and every high thing that exalts itself against the knowledge of God, bringing every thought into captivity to the obedience of Christ.   2 CORINTHIANS 10.5

KeyPoints

_____

_____

_____

_____

_____

_____

_____

_____

_____

A Model for "Thawing the ICE" of a Non-Christian's Heart

Issue summarized
  Q. "What do you mean by that?"
  Q. "If that is the case, then what do you say about …?"
  Q. Point out the KeyPoints you listed in the above space.

Clarify the religion* associated with it (*worldview/philosophy)
  Q. "Upon what authority do you base your opinion?" (= "Why should I believe you?")
  Q. "Are you willing to base your eternal destiny upon your view?"

Expose it for the self-contradicting foolishness that it is.
• Repeat his presuppositions so he can hear how foolish they are
• Since their objection is going to be based upon subjective reasons, relate your questions to objective biblical reasons.
• Contrast its ultimate consequences (a consistent record of failure throughout history) with the historic record of success of communities, states and nations who have followed Christian principles.
• Explain which self-governing sphere(s) should be handling the issue (Individual, Family, Church, State).
• Present a humble, yet bold presentation of the Gospel

WEEK 33
Are you carrying Jesus "on your back," or "inside your heart?"

The following illustration shows how dealing with the "fruit" of the collective non-Christian worldview in which we are currently living will not affect the change in our culture that we desire. To achieve that goal we must deal with the "root" cause.

The "Fruit"

1. Reform Public Schools
2. Promote Christmas
3. Display the Commandments
4. Get the Vote Out
5. Oppose Abortion

Jesus' Backpack

The "Root"

1. Instead of obeying the 1st Commandment to worship only the triune God of Scripture.
2. Instead of objecting to ungodly politically-correct policies (and curriculum).
3. Instead of encouraging churches to counsel (and perhaps discipline) members who are legislators, judges and CEOs for making decisions that do not conform to Scripture.
4. Instead of churches instructing their members in how Christian civil rulers should govern.
5. Instead of promoting the idea that our civil laws should be based upon biblical principles. (or do we want to give the impression that man is smarter than God when it comes to determining how we should live and govern ourselves.)

What must be recognized is that our "Jesus Backpack" mentality conforms to the way non-Christians approach life. For them, there is no definitive way to live, so their worldview and lifestyle is characterized by different aspects of a person's life that are "acted out" in whatever ways are supported by the latest opinion polls.

Rather than attempting to carry Christ around on our back, we need to obey His commands that we carry Him around inside our heart (Jeremiah 24.7; Ezekiel 11.19; Matthew 5.8; 6.21; Colossians 3.15). The difference between these two lifestyles is dramatic:

• If Jesus is in our backpack, we *act* for Him.
• If Jesus is in our heart, we *live* for Him.

IN YOUR OWN WORDS

Casting down arguments and every high thing that exalts itself against the knowledge of God, bringing every thought into captivity to the obedience of Christ.   2 CORINTHIANS 10.5

KeyPoints

_____

_____

_____

_____

_____

_____

_____

_____

_____

A Model for "Thawing the ICE" of a Non-Christian's Heart

Issue summarized
   Q. "What do you mean by that?"
   Q. "If that is the case, then what do you say about …?"
   Q. Point out the KeyPoints you listed in the above space.

Clarify the religion* associated with it (*worldview/philosophy)
   Q. "Upon what authority do you base your opinion?" (= "Why should I believe you?")
   Q. "Are you willing to base your eternal destiny upon your view?"

Expose it for the self-contradicting foolishness that it is.
• Repeat his presuppositions so he can hear how foolish they are
• Since their objection is going to be based upon subjective reasons, relate your questions to objective biblical reasons.
• Contrast its ultimate consequences (a consistent record of failure throughout history) with the historic record of success of communities, states and nations who have followed Christian principles.
• Explain which self-governing sphere(s) should be handling the issue (Individual, Family, Church, State).
• Present a humble, yet bold presentation of the Gospel

WEEK 34
Are you "putting off the old," and "putting on the new?"

The apostle Paul tells us that, as Christians, "the spirit of the world" that we used to have has been replaced with the "Spirit who is from God so that we might know the things that have been freely given to us by God." [1]

? *Explain why you think it is that some of your Christian friends (who, by the very definition of Christianity, "know" the truth) refuse to incorporate biblical principles into their daily decision-making?*

Ask them for their reasons and you will see that they will either be based upon pragmatism, rationalizations, or a misinterpretation of Scripture. Do you think you can assist them in recognizing the need for externalizing their faith? (By the way, how are you doing in "exiting" your beliefs from your home, church and/or small group Bible study?)

? *What message are you sending to non-Christians who observe your daily decisions (which result from your worldview)?*

? *Review your most recent decisions to determine whether they were based upon biblical principles, or non-biblical ones (pragmatism and/or rationalization)?*

? *Ask yourself: "Is this a conservative response to a liberal action, or a Christian response to an ungodly action?"*

In bringing all of this together, it might be helpful to recall that since we are children of God, how does our Father in heaven view our day-to-day decisions? Asked another way: How is it with your children? Would you prefer that they "acted" for you in certain isolated situations because that's what they knew you expected, or would you prefer that they "live" for you in all situations and circumstances because they can't imagine any other acceptable way to live in order to bring "honor" to you? [2]

NOTES
1 2 Corinthians 2.12
2 Exodus 20.12

IN YOUR OWN WORDS

Casting down arguments and every high thing that exalts itself against the knowledge of God, bringing every thought into captivity to the obedience of Christ.   2 CORINTHIANS 10.5

KeyPoints

_____

_____

_____

_____

_____

_____

_____

_____

A Model for "Thawing the ICE" of a Non-Christian's Heart

Issue summarized
  Q. "What do you mean by that?"
  Q. "If that is the case, then what do you say about …?"
  Q. Point out the KeyPoints you listed in the above space.

Clarify the religion* associated with it (*worldview/philosophy)
  Q. "Upon what authority do you base your opinion?" (= "Why should I believe you?")
  Q. "Are you willing to base your eternal destiny upon your view?"

Expose it for the self-contradicting foolishness that it is.
• Repeat his presuppositions so he can hear how foolish they are
• Since their objection is going to be based upon subjective reasons, relate your questions to objective biblical reasons.
• Contrast its ultimate consequences (a consistent record of failure throughout history) with the historic record of success of communities, states and nations who have followed Christian principles.
• Explain which self-governing sphere(s) should be handling the issue (Individual, Family, Church, State).
• Present a humble, yet bold presentation of the Gospel

Why should we be careful to frame culture's debates according to God's Word vs. man's word, instead of according to conservative vs. liberal ideas?

All cultural questions are answered in terms of man's opinion or God's opinion. For Christians, there is no intermediate being that is a combination of man and God. Similarly for non-Christians, who don't believe in the triune God of the Bible, there is only one category: man.

Since God's Word is truth, any decision we make and any action we take that does not conform to Scripture is "false." So when we "compromise God's Word in order to build an alliance with non-Christians, we are dishonoring God by living as though we're smarter than He is in that particular instance.

As the only people who have been enabled by the Holy Spirit to correctly understand God's Word, we are also doing a major disservice to our non-Christian neighbors when we refuse to make decisions that conform to His Word. The reason for this is that we are the only Bible they may "read" and God may be using our testimony in a particular situation or circumstance to convict their heart of the truth for which they have been looking in all the wrong places!

This is why we must always be on our toes to not let non-Christian viruses creep into our worldview and lifestyle. Since only God's Word is true, none of our plans will prove successful unless they reflect His principles.

> *Therefore humble yourselves under the mighty hand of God, that He may exalt you in due time, casting all your care upon Him, for He cares for you.*
>
> *Be sober, be vigilant; because your adversary the devil walks about like a roaring lion, seeking whom he may devour. Resist him, steadfast in the faith, knowing that the same sufferings are experienced by your brotherhood in the world.*   1 Peter 5.6-9

> *Then the LORD spoke to Moses, saying, "Speak to the children of Israel, and say to them: 'I am the LORD your God. According to the doings of the land of Egypt, where you dwell, you shall not do; and according to the doings of the land of Canaan, where I am bringing you, you shall not do; nor shall you walk in their ordinances. You shall observe My judgments and keep My ordinances, to walk in them: I am the LORD your God. You shall therefore keep My statutes and My judgments, which if a man does, he shall live by them: I am the LORD.*   Leviticus 18.1-5

IN YOUR OWN WORDS

Casting down arguments and every high thing that exalts itself against the knowledge of God, bringing every thought into captivity to the obedience of Christ.　　　　　　　　　　　　　　2 CORINTHIANS 10.5

KeyPoints

_____

_____

_____

_____

_____

_____

_____

_____

A Model for "Thawing the ICE" of a Non-Christian's Heart

Issue summarized
- Q. "What do you mean by that?"
- Q. "If that is the case, then what do you say about …?"
- Q. Point out the KeyPoints you listed in the above space.

Clarify the religion* associated with it (*worldview/philosophy)
- Q. "Upon what authority do you base your opinion?" (= "Why should I believe you?")
- Q. "Are you willing to base your eternal destiny upon your view?"

Expose it for the self-contradicting foolishness that it is.
- Repeat his presuppositions so he can hear how foolish they are
- Since their objection is going to be based upon subjective reasons, relate your questions to objective biblical reasons.
- Contrast its ultimate consequences (a consistent record of failure throughout history) with the historic record of success of communities, states and nations who have followed Christian principles.
- Explain which self-governing sphere(s) should be handling the issue (Individual, Family, Church, State).
- Present a humble, yet bold presentation of the Gospel

Why is it said that our true character is revealed in Scripture?

Yes, we make decisions according to our "free will," but the Bible tells us that our will is "free" only to make God-dishonoring decisions. In the inspired words of "the Preacher"

> *God made man upright, but they have sought out many schemes.*
>
> ECCLESIASTES 7.29

Let's go back to the first conversation God had with Noah and his family as they stepped out of the ark and onto dry land:

> *I will never again curse the ground for man's sake, although the imagination of man's heart is evil from his youth.*   GENESIS 8.21

Now, let's fast forward in time to the sixth century B.C. and hear how the prophet Jeremiah describes the human decision-making condition:

> *The heart is deceitful above all things, and desperately wicked; who can know it?*   JEREMIAH 17.9

King Solomon similarly decries

> *Truly the hearts of the sons of men are full of evil; madness is in their hearts ...*
>
> ECCLESIASTES 9.3

If we look to New Testament examples, we will find corroborating statements by Jesus and Paul:

> *For I know that in me (that is, in my flesh) nothing good dwells.*
>
> ROMANS 7.18

Paul continues by stating

> *Because the carnal mind is enmity against God; for it is not subject to the law of God, nor indeed can be. So then, those who are in the flesh cannot please God.*
>
> ROMANS 8.7-8

IN YOUR OWN WORDS

Casting down arguments and every high thing that exalts itself against the knowledge of God, bringing every thought into captivity to the obedience of Christ.   2 CORINTHIANS 10.5

KeyPoints

_____

_____

_____

_____

_____

_____

_____

_____

_____

A Model for "Thawing the ICE" of a Non-Christian's Heart

Issue summarized
  Q. "What do you mean by that?"
  Q. "If that is the case, then what do you say about …?"
  Q. Point out the KeyPoints you listed in the above space.

Clarify the religion* associated with it (*worldview/philosophy)
  Q. "Upon what authority do you base your opinion?" (= "Why should I believe you?")
  Q. "Are you willing to base your eternal destiny upon your view?"

Expose it for the self-contradicting foolishness that it is.
• Repeat his presuppositions so he can hear how foolish they are
• Since their objection is going to be based upon subjective reasons, relate your questions to objective biblical reasons.
• Contrast its ultimate consequences (a consistent record of failure throughout history) with the historic record of success of communities, states and nations who have followed Christian principles.
• Explain which self-governing sphere(s) should be handling the issue (Individual, Family, Church, State).
• Present a humble, yet bold presentation of the Gospel

WEEK 37
Why is it that we can only honor Jesus through our daily decisions and actions?

Obviously, this is not a pretty picture. Indeed, it's a very disturbing one. As Christians, we want to bring honor to Jesus with our decisions, yet throughout Scripture we are told that by depending upon our wisdom, logic and pragmatism, it will be impossible to honor Jesus with any decision we make! Jeremiah characterizes such self-centered thinking by Christians as having their heart "depart from the LORD." [1] Since the only way any of us becomes a Christian is for the Holy Spirit to "write the law upon our hearts," [2] the thought of having our heart "depart from the LORD" should be one that is most unsettling. Isaiah adds this "woe" for those who think their own thoughts:

> *"Woe to the rebellious children," says the LORD, "Who take counsel, but not of Me, and who devise plans, but not of My Spirit, that they may add sin to sin; who walk to go down to Egypt, and have not asked My advice, to strengthen themselves in the strength of Pharaoh, and to trust in the shadow of Egypt! Therefore the strength of Pharaoh shall be your shame, and trust in the shadow of Egypt shall be your humiliation.*   ISAIAH 30.1-3

Notice that Jehovah tells the Israelites that if they want to trust in the wisdom and strength of the state, instead of in His wisdom and strength, then that's exactly what their wisdom and strength shall be and the result will be "humiliation" instead of "holiness." Jesus' half-brother James makes the same point by stating that if we lean on our own wisdom we will be "double-minded" and "unstable in all of our ways." [3]

As these verses teach, the deceitfulness of our sinful heart means that the only way we can be certain that our decisions are "true" and God-honoring is for us to re-think God's thoughts. As Jehovah asks Job: "Who is this who darkens counsel by words without knowledge?" [4] Jehovah's meaning to Job (and the rest of us) is: "You may think that you are smart, but without filtering your thoughts and knowledge through my revealed Word, you are foolish!" We may not like to be reminded of this, and certainly non-Christians would dispute it, but the truth is "if the light that is in us is darkness, then so will our view of the world be 'dark.'" [5] Non-Christians have no excuse for the "darkness" of their worldview, because in their unredeemed state of being separate from God, it's the natural way for them to view things. We, however, know better, and by consistently comparing our decisions to the biblical principles in which we profess to believe, we can keep from falling prey to Satan's temptations to make our decisions based solely upon our wisdom. So, as we approach each decision, may we remind ourselves that it is in "Christ's light that we see light." [6]

NOTES

1 Jeremiah 17.5	3 James 1.8; 4.8	5 Matthew 6.23
2 Jeremiah 31.33	4 Job 38.2	6 Psalm 36.9

IN YOUR OWN WORDS

Casting down arguments and every high thing that exalts itself against the knowledge of God, bringing every thought into captivity to the obedience of Christ.   2 CORINTHIANS 10.5

KeyPoints

_____

_____

_____

_____

_____

_____

_____

_____

_____

A Model for "Thawing the ICE" of a Non-Christian's Heart

Issue summarized
  Q. "What do you mean by that?"
  Q. "If that is the case, then what do you say about …?"
  Q. Point out the KeyPoints you listed in the above space.

Clarify the religion* associated with it (*worldview/philosophy)
  Q. "Upon what authority do you base your opinion?" (= "Why should I believe you?")
  Q. "Are you willing to base your eternal destiny upon your view?"

Expose it for the self-contradicting foolishness that it is.
- Repeat his presuppositions so he can hear how foolish they are
- Since their objection is going to be based upon subjective reasons, relate your questions to objective biblical reasons.
- Contrast its ultimate consequences (a consistent record of failure throughout history) with the historic record of success of communities, states and nations who have followed Christian principles.
- Explain which self-governing sphere(s) should be handling the issue (Individual, Family, Church, State).
- Present a humble, yet bold presentation of the Gospel

WEEK 38
What is wrong with the proposition that there is a "religious" realm and a "real life" realm to life?

One of the most successful tactics that Satan uses to keep us "in our place" (inside our homes and churches) is to propose that "life" is composed of "religious" and "real life" realms. Once we agree with this principle, it's a matter of time until the state declares more and more areas of our life as belonging to the "real life" realm, which serves to prevent us from speaking to the various cultural issues with biblical principles.

God created everything and proclaimed it "good," (Genesis 1.10) therefore every area of life is "religious." Biblically speaking, every area of our life is at once "religious, and "real." The non-Christian worldview is based upon the error of man's opinion, which means that nothing they propose or do is "real." By refusing to believe that God's Word is truth, the only option they have is to make decisions that they think or hope will prove successful in the current "moment!" Yet, history proves that no man-centered civil government has ever succeeded, nor will it ever. On the other hand, history is replete with successful examples of civil governments who based their laws upon biblical principles.

All Christians are quick to say that they believe in God's Word. However, the lifestyles of far too many of our brothers and sisters indicate that they "believe it" only in certain situations and circumstances.

Each of us has been called into Christ's Kingdom to reveal His counsel on how to live to our non-Christian neighbors. Waiting for the climate to "improve," or for "better timing" are lame excuses that serve to hide our disrespect for God's Word, and proves that we are not truly appreciative of His making His will known to us, since we don't think it is worth our time to pass it along to someone else.

As Christians we know of but one realm: Christ's Kingdom, where we are to serve Him in as holy a manner as we can, and that begins with an unequivocal belief in God's Word and an unflinching desire to stand for His ways whenever we can.

Casting down arguments and every high thing that exalts itself against the knowledge of God, bringing every thought into captivity to the obedience of Christ.   2 CORINTHIANS 10.5

Do not be deceived, God is not mocked; for whatever a man sows, that he will also reap.   GALATIANS 6.7

IN YOUR OWN WORDS

Casting down arguments and every high thing that exalts itself against the knowledge of God, bringing every thought into captivity to the obedience of Christ. 2 CORINTHIANS 10.5

KeyPoints

_____

_____

_____

_____

_____

_____

_____

_____

_____

A Model for "Thawing the ICE" of a Non-Christian's Heart

Issue summarized
  Q. "What do you mean by that?"
  Q. "If that is the case, then what do you say about …?"
  Q. Point out the KeyPoints you listed in the above space.

Clarify the religion* associated with it (*worldview/philosophy)
  Q. "Upon what authority do you base your opinion?" (= "Why should I believe you?")
  Q. "Are you willing to base your eternal destiny upon your view?"

Expose it for the self-contradicting foolishness that it is.
• Repeat his presuppositions so he can hear how foolish they are
• Since their objection is going to be based upon subjective reasons, relate your questions to objective biblical reasons.
• Contrast its ultimate consequences (a consistent record of failure throughout history) with the historic record of success of communities, states and nations who have followed Christian principles.
• Explain which self-governing sphere(s) should be handling the issue (Individual, Family, Church, State).
• Present a humble, yet bold presentation of the Gospel

WEEK 39
What does it mean to be "salt and light" to those with whom we come in contact?

> *You are the salt of the earth; but if the salt loses its flavor, how shall it be*
> *seasoned? It is then good for nothing but to be thrown out and trampled*
> *underfoot by men. You are the light of the world. A city that is set on a hill*
> *cannot be hidden. Nor do they light a lamp and put it under a basket, but on*
> *a lamp stand, and it gives light to all who are in the house. Let your light so*
> *shine before men, that they may see your good works and glorify your Father in*
> *heaven.*   MATTHEW 5.13-16

Since being "salt and light" to our communities is our basic calling, anyone who professes to be a Christian and refuses to carry out his calling is "good for nothing," and they and their community (if it also refuses to live by biblical principles) will be "trodden under the foot of men." [1] Only biblical principles, provide the true light through which non-Christians can see their true selves, and come to repentance and a saving knowledge of Christ, and only God's counsel provides the correct way to live and govern ourselves.

In the Old Testament, God's prophets were the "salt" of the land of Canaan, and now we are the "salt" of the entire earth. The gospel acts as salt, being "living and powerful" [2] and it reaches the heart of God's intended hearers. [3]

We who are "light in the Lord" have been called into Christ's Kingdom to illuminate the world, which is living in spiritual darkness.

> *That you may become blameless and harmless, children of God without fault*
> *in the midst of a crooked and perverse generation, among whom you shine as*
> *lights in the world, holding fast the word of life, so that I may rejoice in the day*
> *of Christ that I have not run in vain or labored in vain.*
> 　　　　　　　　　　　　　　　　　　　　　PHILIPPIANS 2.15-16

In all we do and say, bringing glory and honor to Christ should be our top priority. [4]

> *Finally, brothers, whatever things are true, whatever things are noble,*
> *whatever things are just, whatever things are pure, whatever things are*
> *lovely, whatever things are of good report, if there is any virtue and if there is*
> *anything praiseworthy—meditate on these things.*   PHILIPPIANS 4.8

> *Let your speech always be with grace, seasoned with salt, that you may know*
> *how you ought to answer each one.*   COLOSSIANS 4.6

NOTES

1　Matthew 5.13	3　Acts 2.37
2　Hebrews 4.12	4　1 Peter 4.11

IN YOUR OWN WORDS

Casting down arguments and every high thing that exalts itself against the knowledge of God, bringing every thought into captivity to the obedience of Christ.   2 CORINTHIANS 10.5

KeyPoints

_____

_____

_____

_____

_____

_____

_____

_____

_____

A Model for "Thawing the ICE" of a Non-Christian's Heart

Issue summarized
  Q. "What do you mean by that?"
  Q. "If that is the case, then what do you say about …?"
  Q. Point out the KeyPoints you listed in the above space.

Clarify the religion* associated with it (*worldview/philosophy)
  Q. "Upon what authority do you base your opinion?" (= "Why should I believe you?")
  Q. "Are you willing to base your eternal destiny upon your view?"

Expose it for the self-contradicting foolishness that it is.
- Repeat his presuppositions so he can hear how foolish they are
- Since their objection is going to be based upon subjective reasons, relate your questions to objective biblical reasons.
- Contrast its ultimate consequences (a consistent record of failure throughout history) with the historic record of success of communities, states and nations who have followed Christian principles.
- Explain which self-governing sphere(s) should be handling the issue (Individual, Family, Church, State).
- Present a humble, yet bold presentation of the Gospel

AUDIBLE "S"

THE STATE IS EXEMPT FROM GOD'S AUTHORITY

SCOUTING REPORT

Fundamental Points That Can Be Used Successfully Against These "Defenses"

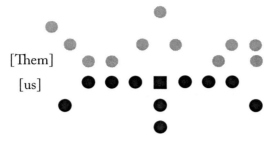

[Them]

[us]

Make Your Reads, and *Believe* What You Know

- Theocracy means "the rule of God" or "the authority of God." Those who deny the authority of God's laws toward their culture because "the Jews lived under a theocracy and therefore cannot be an example to us," should understand that when they pick up one end of that stick, they pick up both ends. To dismiss God's civil advice to the Old Testament kings is to also dismiss His personal advice, since it is one and the same code of conduct! If taken to its logical conclusion, this type of thinking would nullify the lessons of the entire Old Testament!

- The Church excommunicates disobedient members as a last resort. The State executes criminals convicted of capital crimes as a last resort. While repentance can restore a person to church membership, it cannot remove the punishment due a civic crime. As the examples of Sodom and Gomorrah and Ninevah attest, even citizens of non-Christian nations are obliged to keep God's civil laws.

- Pluralism sees all religions more or less the same. Obviously this attitude breaks the first commandment to "have no other gods before Me." (Exodus 20.3) It is also important to understand that it is impossible for any society to be governed by more than one set of ethics. Either God's ethics will be accepted, or man's. Either man determines the civil laws, and their rewards and punishments, or God does. Our only choice is to be ruled by God's absolute, unchanging, and personally liberating ethics or by man's ever-changing, tyrannical, and enslaving ethics.

- It is impossible to separate "religion" from the state's realm. "Religion" after all, is simply a set of ethics by which one lives his life. Therefore, all civil governments are based upon the "religious" ideas of its office holders. The question is which "religion" is reflected in the civil laws: man's or God's. What good does it do for a community to believe in one set of beliefs, yet live by a civil law-code that contradicts those beliefs?

- There is certainly no doubt about the Bible teaching that we should "render to Caesar what is Caesar's," but in obeying this command of Jesus we need to be careful that we are not "rendering to Caesar more that he is due," for that would also be a sin.

WEEK 40
Why should civil laws conform to biblical laws, since modern nations are not in covenant with God?

One doesn't have to read far in Genesis to find that God consistently uses His law as a standard of judgment to Canaanite and pagan rulers who were not in covenant with Him. The truth is that God is holy and desires for us to be holy. The only way for us to accomplish this is to obey His laws, since they describe how He wishes everyone to live. The law was given to Israel to show other governments its righteousness. This is what Moses taught the Israelites concerning their entrance into the Promised Land:

> *Now, O Israel, listen to the statutes and judgments which I teach you to observe that you may go in and possess the land which the Lord God of your fathers is giving you. You shall not add to the word which I command you, nor take from it, that you may keep the commandments of the Lord your God which I command you.* DEUTERONOMY 4.1-2

Leviticus 18.24-27 demonstrates that God never had a double standard...one for Israel and another for the rest of the world. As the Israelites were gathered in the wilderness, the Lord spoke these instructions to Moses:

> *For the land is defiled; therefore I visit the punishment of its iniquity upon it, and the land vomits out its inhabitants. You shall therefore keep My statutes and My judgments, and shall not commit any of these abominations ...*

In the New Testament we hear Paul telling the Corinthians not to be drunk, so does that mean its alright for people in your state to be drunk? Certainly not. The principles in Corinthians and in Romans 1 and 2 apply to all people. Genesis 19 describes the unrighteous and sinful people of Sodom, and Peter describes how God delivered righteous Lot from their filthy conduct. As King Solomon proclaims, "righteousness exalts a nation, but sin is a reproach to any people." [1] Paul describes those who live "according to the flesh," instead of "according to the Spirit" as having a "carnal mind." [2] James adds, "What does it profit if someone says he has faith but does not have works?" [3] The "works" of which James is speaking, and the only "works" that God declares as "good" are those that conform to His Word.

NOTES
1 Proverbs 14.34
2 Romans 8.6-7
3 James 2.14

IN YOUR OWN WORDS

Casting down arguments and every high thing that exalts itself against the knowledge of God, bringing every thought into captivity to the obedience of Christ.   2 CORINTHIANS 10.5

KeyPoints

_____

_____

_____

_____

_____

_____

_____

_____

_____

A Model for "Thawing the ICE" of a Non-Christian's Heart

Issue summarized
  Q. "What do you mean by that?"
  Q. "If that is the case, then what do you say about …?"
  Q. Point out the KeyPoints you listed in the above space.

Clarify the religion* associated with it (*worldview/philosophy)
  Q. "Upon what authority do you base your opinion?" (= "Why should I believe you?")
  Q. "Are you willing to base your eternal destiny upon your view?"

Expose it for the self-contradicting foolishness that it is.
• Repeat his presuppositions so he can hear how foolish they are
• Since their objection is going to be based upon subjective reasons, relate your questions to objective biblical reasons.
• Contrast its ultimate consequences (a consistent record of failure throughout history) with the historic record of success of communities, states and nations who have followed Christian principles.
• Explain which self-governing sphere(s) should be handling the issue (Individual, Family, Church, State).
• Present a humble, yet bold presentation of the Gospel

Haven't civil sanctions been taken away with the Ceremonial Laws?
Or "The Old Testament penal sanctions were covered in the Crucifixion
of Christ." Or "The Old Testament civil penalties will all be covered in
the final judgment." (Part One)

This objection presupposes that the Old Testament Civil Laws were indistinguishable to the Ceremonial Laws. Those who make this objection reason: "Since the Ceremonial Laws all pointed toward Jesus, and since He fulfilled them by living a perfectly obedient life, dying, and overcoming death, the Old Testament Civil Laws have also been abolished." There is only one flaw in this otherwise tidy argument: There was always a separation (or distinction) between Ceremonial Laws and Civil Laws. Why else would God cause the prophet Hosea to say "I desire faithful love (civil and moral obedience to My laws), not sacrifice (mere ceremonial observances)." [1]

In the civil arena (everyday life) the Jews and Gentiles were accountable for not killing each other, [2] yet in the ecclesiastical arena only the Jews were held accountable for observing certain dietary laws. [3] In addition, there were commands that were specific to

- Kings   Proverbs 31.4-5
- Judges   Deuteronomy 16.18-19
- Parents   Deuteronomy 6.7-9
- Merchants   Leviticus 19.36
- Farmers   Leviticus 19.8-10
- Children   Exodus 20.12
- Priests   Leviticus 1.5

Moreover, it is theologically incredible to imagine that Christ came to make it morally acceptable for man to blaspheme, murder, rape, steal, gossip, or envy! God explicitly forbids kings to swerve to the right or to the left from the well-defined path of His law. 4 There must be a defining limit upon "the things that belong to Caesar." [5] The truth is that unjust Civil Rulers come under God's curse: "Woe to those who enact evil statutes."[6]

The way Paul looked upon the civil magistrate, even the evil emperor of Rome, was that he should behave as "a minister of God" [7] who "avenges wrath against evildoers." In this passage the "vengeance" is clearly intended to be God's, [8] and accordingly, "evil" is defined by the law of God [9] … the magistrate will need the law of God to inform him as to how and where God's wrath is to be worked out in the state.

NOTES
1 Hosea 6.6
2 Leviticus 24.21-22
3 Deuteronomy 14.21
4 Deuteronomy 17.18-20
5 Romans 13.7
6 Isaiah 10.1; Revelation 13.16-17
7 Romans 13.4
8 Romans 12.19; 1 Peter 2.14
9 Romans13.8-10

IN YOUR OWN WORDS

Casting down arguments and every high thing that exalts itself against the knowledge of God, bringing every thought into captivity to the obedience of Christ. 2 CORINTHIANS 10.5

KeyPoints

_____

_____

_____

_____

_____

_____

_____

_____

_____

A Model for "Thawing the ICE" of a Non-Christian's Heart

Issue summarized
  Q. "What do you mean by that?"
  Q. "If that is the case, then what do you say about …?"
  Q. Point out the KeyPoints you listed in the above space.

Clarify the religion* associated with it (*worldview/philosophy)
  Q. "Upon what authority do you base your opinion?" (= "Why should I believe you?")
  Q. "Are you willing to base your eternal destiny upon your view?"

Expose it for the self-contradicting foolishness that it is.
• Repeat his presuppositions so he can hear how foolish they are
• Since their objection is going to be based upon subjective reasons, relate your questions to objective biblical reasons.
• Contrast its ultimate consequences (a consistent record of failure throughout history) with the historic record of success of communities, states and nations who have followed Christian principles.
• Explain which self-governing sphere(s) should be handling the issue (Individual, Family, Church, State).
• Present a humble, yet bold presentation of the Gospel

WEEK 42
Haven't civil sanctions been taken away with the Ceremonial Laws?
Or "The Old Testament penal sanctions were covered in the Crucifixion
of Christ." Or "The Old Testament civil penalties will all be covered in
the final judgment. (Part Two)

There is no better political standard to offer than God's law. Without it we are left with either criminal anarchy or arbitrary and manipulative penalties determined by tyrannical civil rulers. [1] Besides, if the State were truly "neutral," it would enact no laws, for each law would penalize someone's religion or religious view or religious practice. In other words anarchy would reign.

Through His perfect life and cruel death on the Cross, Christ paid our eternal debt, not our civic debt. Otherwise no civil penalty could be assessed against us ... even for a minor traffic violation! Certainly this suggestion cannot be taken seriously, since it would result in no civil penalties for any crimes until Judgment day!

The purpose of law as it relates to the civil magistrate is to punish and restrain evil, to protect human life and property, to provide justice for all people, and to promote good deeds using God's Word as the standard.

Today, it is fashionable to imagine that "Reason is the sovereign of the world," and that "Law is what the state says it is." [2] Legal positivism (i.e., that there is no reason, right or truth apart from the state) is a direct ancestor of the philosophy popularized by 18th century German, Georg Wilhelm Hegel. Non-Christians view the law as evolving, just as they imagine man to be. In direct contrast to this type of thinking is the biblical exclamation of Isaiah:

> *To the law and to the testimony: if they speak not according to this word, it is*
> *because there is no light in them.*　　　　　　　　　　　　Isaiah 8.20

God's law reflects His absolute and unchanging holiness. [3] It is "good" simply because it reflects how the Creator prefers His creatures to live. It is also significant that the New Testament never criticizes the moral demands of Old Testament law. [4]

NOTES
1　Matthew 15.3-5
2　Georg Wilhelm Hegel
3　Romans 7.12; 1 Peter 1.14-16
4　Matthew 4.4

IN YOUR OWN WORDS

Casting down arguments and every high thing that exalts itself against the knowledge of God, bringing every thought into captivity to the obedience of Christ. 2 CORINTHIANS 10.5

KeyPoints

_____

_____

_____

_____

_____

_____

_____

_____

_____

A Model for "Thawing the ICE" of a Non-Christian's Heart

Issue summarized
  Q. "What do you mean by that?"
  Q. "If that is the case, then what do you say about …?"
  Q. Point out the KeyPoints you listed in the above space.

Clarify the religion* associated with it (*worldview/philosophy)
  Q. "Upon what authority do you base your opinion?" (= "Why should I believe you?")
  Q. "Are you willing to base your eternal destiny upon your view?"

Expose it for the self-contradicting foolishness that it is.
• Repeat his presuppositions so he can hear how foolish they are
• Since their objection is going to be based upon subjective reasons, relate your questions to objective biblical reasons.
• Contrast its ultimate consequences (a consistent record of failure throughout history) with the historic record of success of communities, states and nations who have followed Christian principles.
• Explain which self-governing sphere(s) should be handling the issue (Individual, Family, Church, State).
• Present a humble, yet bold presentation of the Gospel

Doesn't excommunication take the place of civil sanctions?

Those who voice this objection overlook the fact that there have always been separate functions for the Church and State. The prophet Zechariah's statement: "These are the two anointed ones, who stand beside the Lord of the whole earth." (ZECHARIAH 4.14)(Joshua the high priest and Zerrabbel the king) The "two anointed ones" refer to the Kings and Priests, as the following brief list illustrates:

KING	PRIEST
Moses	Aaron
Joshua	Eleazar
David	Abiathar
Solomon	Zadok
Hezekiah	Azariah
Zerubbabel	Joshua

The Chronicler makes a similar statement:

> *And take notice: Amariah the chief priest is over you in all matters of the LORD; and Zebadiah the son of Ishmael, the ruler of the house of Judah, for all the king's matters.* 2 CHRONICLES 19.11

The Church excommunicates disobedient members as a last resort. The State executes criminals as a last resort. While repentance can restore a person to church membership, it cannot remove the punishment due a civil crime. As the examples of Sodom and Gomorrah and Ninevah attest, even citizens of non-Christian nations are obliged to keep God's civil laws.

In addition, this objection also erroneously lumps non-Christians in with Christians. How could it be expected that someone who is not a Church member could be excommunicated?

> *Also in the third year of his reign he sent his leaders, Ben-Hail, Obadiah, Zechariah, Nethanel, and Michaiah, to teach in the cities of Judah. And with them he sent Levites: Shemaiah, Nethaniah, Zebadiah, Asahel, Shemiramoth, Jehonathan, Adonijah, Tobijah, and Tobadonijah—the Levites; and with them Elishama and Jehoram, the priests. So they taught in Judah, and had the Book of the Law of the LORD with them; they went throughout all the cities of Judah and taught the people.* 2 CHRONICLES 17.7-9

IN YOUR OWN WORDS

Casting down arguments and every high thing that exalts itself against the knowledge of God, bringing every thought into captivity to the obedience of Christ.   2 CORINTHIANS 10.5

KeyPoints

_____

_____

_____

_____

_____

_____

_____

_____

_____

A Model for "Thawing the ICE" of a Non-Christian's Heart

Issue summarized
  Q. "What do you mean by that?"
  Q. "If that is the case, then what do you say about …?"
  Q. Point out the KeyPoints you listed in the above space.

Clarify the religion* associated with it (*worldview/philosophy)
  Q. "Upon what authority do you base your opinion?" (= "Why should I believe you?")
  Q. "Are you willing to base your eternal destiny upon your view?"

Expose it for the self-contradicting foolishness that it is.
* Repeat his presuppositions so he can hear how foolish they are
* Since their objection is going to be based upon subjective reasons, relate your questions to objective biblical reasons.
* Contrast its ultimate consequences (a consistent record of failure throughout history) with the historic record of success of communities, states and nations who have followed Christian principles.
* Explain which self-governing sphere(s) should be handling the issue (Individual, Family, Church, State).
* Present a humble, yet bold presentation of the Gospel

WEEK 44
The apostle Paul states that "the weapons of our warfare are not carnal but mighty in God for pulling down strongholds," (2 Corinthians 10.4) so shouldn't we limit our activities to witnessing and prayer and leave the civil government to non-Christians?

Some use these words by Paul to intimate that he was teaching some kind of a rebellion against the civil government. However, such attempts are quickly shown to be false once the context of this passage is considered. The truth is that Paul was addressing Church, not civil matters.

Christianity, distinctly unlike other religions, never uses carnal means such as physical coercion to convict, convert and discipline sinners. This point is obvious from verse five where Paul says that the churches are used to cast down arguments. We are to bring "every thought into captivity to the obedience of Christ." [1] Spiritual ends require spiritual means.

Paul later says that we, as Christian soldiers, should take up the "whole armor of God," which includes the "helmet of salvation, and the sword of the Spirit, which is the word of God." [2] In a similar manner James talks about "pleasures that war in our members," [3] and Peter mentions "fleshly lusts which war against the soul." [4]

What is being said here is that we have the tremendous advantage and benefit of being able to communicate our requests and petitions to the Creator God of the universe and it is this power, rather than man-made resources that we can depend upon and trust-in to bring us success against our persecutors. A verse similar to this is recorded by the prophet Zechariah as he quotes Jehovah:

> *"Not by might nor by power, but by My Spirit," says the Lord of hosts.*
> ZECHARIAH 4.6

To those who say that this verse implies that Christians should limit our activities to witnessing and prayer, while leaving civil government to the direction of non-Christians, we should ask them to stop ignoring history. The historical setting of this verse was that the Jews had recently returned from Babylonian captivity and they wanted to rebuild their Temple. In every sense of the phrase, they were a rag-tag outfit poorly equipped and surrounded by powerful enemies. Zechariah's words, then, were meant to comfort the Jews, assuring them that Jehovah would provide any "might" and "power" they lacked through His Spirit, as they re-built the Temple. There is nothing here concerning the day-to-day operation of civil government (although it is mercifully and graciously true that His Spirit guides us in all our endeavors).

NOTES

1 2 Corinthians 10.5
2 Ephesians 6.11-17

3 James 4.1
4 1 Peter 2.11

IN YOUR OWN WORDS

Casting down arguments and every high thing that exalts itself against the knowledge of God, bringing every thought into captivity to the obedience of Christ. 2 CORINTHIANS 10.5

KeyPoints

_____

_____

_____

_____

_____

_____

_____

_____

_____

_____

A Model for "Thawing the ICE" of a Non-Christian's Heart

Issue summarized
  Q. "What do you mean by that?"
  Q. "If that is the case, then what do you say about …?"
  Q. Point out the KeyPoints you listed in the above space.

Clarify the religion* associated with it (*worldview/philosophy)
  Q. "Upon what authority do you base your opinion?" (= "Why should I believe you?")
  Q. "Are you willing to base your eternal destiny upon your view?"

Expose it for the self-contradicting foolishness that it is.
• Repeat his presuppositions so he can hear how foolish they are
• Since their objection is going to be based upon subjective reasons, relate your questions to objective biblical reasons.
• Contrast its ultimate consequences (a consistent record of failure throughout history) with the historic record of success of communities, states and nations who have followed Christian principles.
• Explain which self-governing sphere(s) should be handling the issue (Individual, Family, Church, State).
• Present a humble, yet bold presentation of the Gospel

What's the difference between the terms, "Kingdom of God,"
"Kingdom of Heaven," and "Kingdom of Christ?" Do they refer
to three different "Kingdoms?"

All three of these terms can be confusing, but they refer to the Mediatory Kingdom of Christ, to which all Christians belong while they are on the earth. When He exorcised demons, Jesus said that the Kingdom had come. [1] Satan, while defeated by Christ's perfect lifestyle and obedience to the will of God the Father, is currently "bound" [2] which means that our duty is to bring this defeat to completion. Christ has made us a kingdom of priests to God and our Father. [3] The Kingdom is not the church, but it creates the church and works through the church.

In the meantime, Christ leaves no doubt that He is in complete control of His creation:

> *All the ends of the world shall remember and turn to the LORD: and all the*
> *kindreds of the nations shall worship before You. For the Kingdom is the*
> *LORD's; and He is the governor among the nations.* PSALM 22.27-28

Once Jesus makes His triumphant return in judgment, He will give the Kingdom to God the Father where we will all be members of His Consummate Kingdom throughout eternity. So, it's helpful to keep in mind that if a prophecy concerning the Kingdom refers to something happening in time, then it is referring to Christ's Kingdom. On the other hand, if the prophecy is referring to eternity, then it is referring to God the Father's Kingdom.

When this present stage of the Kingdom has been completed and Christ's whole work of redemption has been accomplished, He will turn the Kingdom over to the Father, and then the triune God will reign throughout eternity in the perfect Consummate Kingdom.

> *And when all things have been subjected to Him, then shall the Son also Himself*
> *be subject to Him that did subject all things to Him, that God may be all in all.*
> 1 CORINTHIANS 15.28

When Jesus was being tempted by Satan, Matthew and Luke tell us that He was "taken to a high mountain and shown the kingdoms of the world" that belonged to Satan. [4] Satan has "blinded the minds" of non-Christians, [5] but as soon as the Holy Spirit implants a new spiritual heart in them, the "veil is lifted" from their eyes and Satan no longer has any power over them. [6]

NOTES

1 Matthew 12.28; Luke 17.21
2 Matthew 12.29
3 Revelation 1.6
4 Matthew 4.8; Luke 4.5

5 2 Corinthians 4.4
6 John 3.3, 5; 2 Corinthians 3.14; Romans 14.17; Colossians 1.13

IN YOUR OWN WORDS

Casting down arguments and every high thing that exalts itself against the knowledge of God, bringing every thought into captivity to the obedience of Christ.   2 CORINTHIANS 10.5

KeyPoints

_____

_____

_____

_____

_____

_____

_____

_____

_____

A Model for "Thawing the ICE" of a Non-Christian's Heart

Issue summarized
  Q. "What do you mean by that?"
  Q. "If that is the case, then what do you say about ...?"
  Q. Point out the KeyPoints you listed in the above space.

Clarify the religion* associated with it (*worldview/philosophy)
  Q. "Upon what authority do you base your opinion?" (= "Why should I believe you?")
  Q. "Are you willing to base your eternal destiny upon your view?"

Expose it for the self-contradicting foolishness that it is.
  • Repeat his presuppositions so he can hear how foolish they are
  • Since their objection is going to be based upon subjective reasons, relate your questions to objective biblical reasons.
  • Contrast its ultimate consequences (a consistent record of failure throughout history) with the historic record of success of communities, states and nations who have followed Christian principles.
  • Explain which self-governing sphere(s) should be handling the issue (Individual, Family, Church, State).
  • Present a humble, yet bold presentation of the Gospel

WEEK 46
How can you possibly say with a straight face that all law is "religious?"

This is a very common objection and there is only one thing wrong with it: It's completely unbiblical! The truth of the matter is that it is impossible to separate "religion" from the state's realm. "Religion" after all, is simply a set of ethics by which one lives. Therefore, all civil governments are based upon the "religious" ideas of its office holders. The question is which "religion" is reflected in the civil laws: Man's or God's.

The first place to begin in addressing this statement is to ask the objector to define the word, "religion." He may reply, "I am talking about 'laws,' not 'religions.'" Your response could be: "What are a civilization's laws based upon?" Most likely the objector will say, "Whatever principles the citizens agree upon as to 'good and bad' behavior." Your response is: "But isn't that the same definition of a religion? … What else is a 'religion' but a set of commonly held beliefs? And what good does is do for a community to believe in one set of beliefs, yet live by a civil law-code that contradicts those beliefs?"

Someone may object, "Wait a minute! Law is law and religion is religion." But when it is remembered a religion is simply a system of beliefs and values and a society's laws reflect that system of beliefs, it will be seen that law is inescapably religious. For example, should a person's property be taxed? In order to answer that it must be asked: "Who owns it, God or the State?" It's a religious question! So, if the source of law is man's reason, then man's reason is the god of that society.

Isn't it interesting that the State is doing the very thing it warns might happen if God's principles were brought into their decision making! While telling us, "You shouldn't legislate morality!" non-Christian legislators are doing the exact thing through their laws.

Our culture battle is not between conservative ideas and liberal ideas. It's between Christian ideas and non-Christian ideas. We must be ever conscious that we are operating in His world and that our efforts will fail unless we consistently live by His rules. Piecemeal obedience will not enable us, or communities, our state, or America to be the recipients of God's promised blessings.

> *We should no longer be children, tossed to and fro and carried about with every wind of doctrine, by the trickery of men, in the cunning craftiness of deceitful plotting.*　　EPHESIANS 4.14

> *Do not be carried about by various and strange doctrines.*　　HEBREWS 13.9

IN YOUR OWN WORDS

Casting down arguments and every high thing that exalts itself against the knowledge of God, bringing every thought into captivity to the obedience of Christ. 2 CORINTHIANS 10.5

KeyPoints

_____

_____

_____

_____

_____

_____

_____

_____

_____

A Model for "Thawing the ICE" of a Non-Christian's Heart

Issue summarized
  Q. "What do you mean by that?"
  Q. "If that is the case, then what do you say about ...?"
  Q. Point out the KeyPoints you listed in the above space.

Clarify the religion* associated with it (*worldview/philosophy)
  Q. "Upon what authority do you base your opinion?" (= "Why should I believe you?")
  Q. "Are you willing to base your eternal destiny upon your view?"

Expose it for the self-contradicting foolishness that it is.
* Repeat his presuppositions so he can hear how foolish they are
* Since their objection is going to be based upon subjective reasons, relate your questions to objective biblical reasons.
* Contrast its ultimate consequences (a consistent record of failure throughout history) with the historic record of success of communities, states and nations who have followed Christian principles.
* Explain which self-governing sphere(s) should be handling the issue (Individual, Family, Church, State).
* Present a humble, yet bold presentation of the Gospel

WEEK 47
Doesn't Jesus teach that we must "Render to Caesar what is Caesar's?"

There is certainly no doubt about our obligation to do this, but in obeying this command of Jesus we need to be careful that we are not "rendering to Caesar more that he is due," for that would also be a sin. The State has the God-given power to use the sword to defend its citizens from outside aggression, 1 and to keep us safe from criminals by administering swift justice according to the sure and certain terms of Biblical law. 2

21st century America has not paid much attention to the God-assigned responsibilities of the four self-governing spheres of Individual, Family, Church and State. The result is that these self-governing spheres have abdicated many of their responsibilities to the State, which the State has gladly accepted (along with our tax money to pay for them!). So instead of paying a combined total of less than 10 percent of our net income to the State,[3] as the Bible teaches, we pay upwards of 40 percent!

Does this mean that Christians should refuse to pay these taxes? Certainly not. We are to obey our civil rulers, but at the same time we should be electing Christian civil rulers who will vote to do away with the taxes on social services, education, and all other services that the self-governing spheres of the Individual, Family and Church should be providing.

Let's look at a few of the similarities and differences between the self-governing spheres of the Church and the State:

SIMILARITIES between Church & State
1. They are both from God and are "ministers of God" and shall give account of their administrations to God.
2. Both must observe the law and commandments of God and each has specific directions from Scripture to guide them.
3. Both are "fathers" and ought to be honored and obeyed according to the principles in the fifth commandment.
4. Both are appointed for the glory of God and the good of mankind.
5. Both compliment each other.

As far as their DIFFERENCES
1. In their ultimate goal, the Civil Rulers bring about temporal peace; the Church offers salvation and eternal peace.
2. The State executes capitol offenders; the Church excommunicates unrepentant and disobedient members.

NOTES
1 Romans 13.1-7
2 Deuteronomy 16.20; Proverbs 21.3
3 1 Samuel 8.11-18

IN YOUR OWN WORDS

Casting down arguments and every high thing that exalts itself against the knowledge of God, bringing every thought into captivity to the obedience of Christ.   2 CORINTHIANS 10.5

KeyPoints

_____

_____

_____

_____

_____

_____

_____

_____

_____

A Model for "Thawing the ICE" of a Non-Christian's Heart

Issue summarized
   Q. "What do you mean by that?"
   Q. "If that is the case, then what do you say about …?"
   Q. Point out the KeyPoints you listed in the above space.

Clarify the religion* associated with it (*worldview/philosophy)
   Q. "Upon what authority do you base your opinion?" (= "Why should I believe you?")
   Q. "Are you willing to base your eternal destiny upon your view?"

Expose it for the self-contradicting foolishness that it is.
•   Repeat his presuppositions so he can hear how foolish they are
•   Since their objection is going to be based upon subjective reasons, relate your questions to objective biblical reasons.
•   Contrast its ultimate consequences (a consistent record of failure throughout history) with the historic record of success of communities, states and nations who have followed Christian principles.
•   Explain which self-governing sphere(s) should be handling the issue (Individual, Family, Church, State).
•   Present a humble, yet bold presentation of the Gospel

Since the "Jewish church was a theocracy," and since "Israel, as a nation, was a type of the church," doesn't that mean that any civil laws that applied to Israel should today be applied to the church?

Those who raise this objection are saying that Israel had no separation or distinction between functions of the Church and the State. Such an assertion is completely without a biblical basis. As discussed, the state is one of four God-ordained self-governing spheres (the other three being the individual, family and the church). By definition a theocracy is a community that establishes its laws according to the laws of God. Jesus tells us that His Kingdom "has come," [1] which means we are supposed to live our lives according to His rules, not our own. To live by any other set of rules is a violation of the first commandment to have "no other Gods before us." [2]

For a Christian to live out of conformity to God's laws is blasphemy. Our calling is to conform the world to God's ways, not ourselves to the world's ways. [3] Scripture teaches, and history proves, that it is impossible for a civilization to sustain itself when its laws are based on a plurality of gods. The only ethical code (civil law code) that has a proven record of success throughout history is the biblical one. So, when someone objects that our current civil government is not theocratic, we should elect representatives who will eliminate ungodly laws, and replace them with ones that conform to biblical ethics.

Biblical ethics are always "in season." As Leviticus 26 and Deuteronomy 28 teach, we will be blessed when we obey His instructions, and cursed when we disobey them. Is this not exactly what the apostle Paul teaches regarding the applicability of the Old Testament? [4]

> *All Scripture is given by inspiration of God, and is profitable for doctrine, for reproof, for correction, for instruction in righteousness, that the man of God may be complete, thoroughly equipped for every good work.*
> 2 TIMOTHY 3.16-17

We must recognize that we must be willing to forsake everything in order to follow Jesus. [5] As Jesus teaches:

> *But he who received seed on the good ground is he who hears the word and understands it, who indeed bears fruit and produces: some a hundredfold, some sixty, some thirty.*
> MATTHEW 13.23

NOTES
1 Matthew 3.2
2 Exodus 20.3
3 Romans 12.2
4 1 Corinthians 10.6-11
5 Luke 14.33

IN YOUR OWN WORDS

Casting down arguments and every high thing that exalts itself against the knowledge of God, bringing every thought into captivity to the obedience of Christ.　　　　2 CORINTHIANS 10.5

KeyPoints

_____

_____

_____

_____

_____

_____

_____

_____

_____

A Model for "Thawing the ICE" of a Non-Christian's Heart

Issue summarized
  Q. "What do you mean by that?"
  Q. "If that is the case, then what do you say about …?"
  Q. Point out the KeyPoints you listed in the above space.

Clarify the religion* associated with it (*worldview/philosophy)
  Q. "Upon what authority do you base your opinion?" (= "Why should I believe you?")
  Q. "Are you willing to base your eternal destiny upon your view?"

Expose it for the self-contradicting foolishness that it is.
• Repeat his presuppositions so he can hear how foolish they are
• Since their objection is going to be based upon subjective reasons, relate your questions to objective biblical reasons.
• Contrast its ultimate consequences (a consistent record of failure throughout history) with the historic record of success of communities, states and nations who have followed Christian principles.
• Explain which self-governing sphere(s) should be handling the issue (Individual, Family, Church, State).
• Present a humble, yet bold presentation of the Gospel

What you are advocating amounts to "blind obedience" to Civil Rulers and couldn't this lead to the State promoting a false religion?

This objection describes the situation that could happen under any form of civil government. Civil Rulers govern according to their worldview, and if that view happens to be non-Christian, their policies and legal decisions will promote a false religion. There is no mention in Scripture about a civil government being pluralistic in its religion. [1] In short, civil rulers are not free to determine the penalties for certain crimes. This is why the godly King Jehoshaphat instructed his judges to

> *Take heed to what you are doing, for you do not judge for man but for the LORD, who is with you in the judgment.* 2 CHRONICLES 19.6

This also explains why the psalmist proclaims to civil rulers:

> *Now therefore, be wise, O kings; be instructed, you judges of the earth. Serve the LORD with fear, and rejoice with trembling. Kiss the Son, lest He be angry, and you perish in the way, when His wrath is kindled but a little. Blessed are all those who put their trust in Him.* PSALM 2.10-12

Therefore in submitting to civil rulers who are enforcing God's rules, we should also resist those who are enforcing man's rules. As long, then, as civil rulers enforce God's rules, instead of making up rules (laws) of their own, citizens have no option but to obey them. What this means is that in order to properly function as God's ministers, civil rulers should be familiar with and study God's Word so they can carry out His will for their citizenry (promoting peace and keeping their community safe). In the words of Samuel: "He that rules over men must be just, ruling in the fear of God." [2]

Tyranny exists when the civil governor "replaces God's laws with his own. Since tyranny is Satanic, not to resist ungodly rulers is to resist God, or expressing this in positive terms, to resist tyranny is to honor God. In addition, since civil rulers are granted power conditionally by the voters, it follows that the people have the power to withdraw their sanction if the conditions are not fulfilled. The biblical way to resist tyrannical civil government is orderly, through "lesser magistrates," instead of individually, which could lead to anarchy and chaos. So, for example, if we have a local problem with the mayor, we should approach a city council member and request that he take our grievance to the mayor.

NOTES
1 Exodus 20.3
2 2 Samuel 23.3

IN YOUR OWN WORDS

Casting down arguments and every high thing that exalts itself against the knowledge of God, bringing every thought into captivity to the obedience of Christ. 2 CORINTHIANS 10.5

KeyPoints

_____

_____

_____

_____

_____

_____

_____

_____

A Model for "Thawing the ICE" of a Non-Christian's Heart

Issue summarized
Q. "What do you mean by that?"
Q. "If that is the case, then what do you say about …?"
Q. Point out the KeyPoints you listed in the above space.

Clarify the religion* associated with it (*worldview/philosophy)
Q. "Upon what authority do you base your opinion?" (= "Why should I believe you?")
Q. "Are you willing to base your eternal destiny upon your view?"

Expose it for the self-contradicting foolishness that it is.
• Repeat his presuppositions so he can hear how foolish they are
• Since their objection is going to be based upon subjective reasons, relate your questions to objective biblical reasons.
• Contrast its ultimate consequences (a consistent record of failure throughout history) with the historic record of success of communities, states and nations who have followed Christian principles.
• Explain which self-governing sphere(s) should be handling the issue (Individual, Family, Church, State).
• Present a humble, yet bold presentation of the Gospel

WEEK 50
Are you not aware that religion and politics don't mix?

The decisions politicians make have a major impact on how we live. After all, it is they who set the standards on what is a crime, how much we are taxed, and so on, and to allow them to determine which actions are acceptable behavior without referring to God's inerrant Word is to invite subjective (and ever-changing) laws as well as subjective and unpredictable judicial verdicts. Only God's Word provides a fixed, never-changing, and predictable ethical standard by which we can confidently strive to live. In addition, without civil law being based upon biblical principles, a community has no "higher authority" to which it can appeal certain judicial decisions. Merely appealing to a higher court of law, still keeps a creature in charge, and since we are all creatures, this may promote physical violence among those who disagree with certain laws. However, when the civil law code is based upon biblical principles, appeals can be made to Scripture, and therefore be peaceful (even if contentious).

The person making this objection should be asked to reconcile the following seven Scriptural facts:

1. Civil government was begun by God giving Noah authority to execute murderers. Genesis 9.6-7
2. Joseph is made ruler in Egypt. Genesis 41.38-49
3. Moses was the civil ruler in Israel, and because of Jethro's counsel, appointed lesser magistrates. Exodus 18.13-27
4. "Case laws" are provided for the government of family, Church and State. Exodus 21 – 23
5. God instructs both priests and kings to follow His law. Deuteronomy 17.14-20
6. The book of Judges is filled with examples of civil rulers delivering Israel from political oppression. Othniel 3.9; Ehud 3.15; Shamgar 3.31; Deborah/Barak 4.4,6; Gideon 6.11; Jephthah 11.1; and Samson 14.1
7. The book of Hebrews commends these civil rulers with the words: "And what more shall I say? For time will fail me if I tell of Gideon, Barak, Samson, Jephthah, of David and Samuel and the prophets who by faith conquered kingdoms, [and] per formed acts or righteousness …" Hebrews 13.32-33

The LORD said to my Lord, "Sit at My right hand, till I make Your enemies Your footstool."
PSALM 110.1; ACTS 2.34-35

Occupy till I return.
LUKE 19.13

IN YOUR OWN WORDS

Casting down arguments and every high thing that exalts itself against the knowledge of God, bringing every thought into captivity to the obedience of Christ.   2 CORINTHIANS 10.5

KeyPoints

_____

_____

_____

_____

_____

_____

_____

_____

_____

A Model for "Thawing the ICE" of a Non-Christian's Heart

Issue summarized
  Q. "What do you mean by that?"
  Q. "If that is the case, then what do you say about …?"
  Q. Point out the KeyPoints you listed in the above space.

Clarify the religion* associated with it (*worldview/philosophy)
  Q. "Upon what authority do you base your opinion?" (= "Why should I believe you?")
  Q. "Are you willing to base your eternal destiny upon your view?"

Expose it for the self-contradicting foolishness that it is.
• Repeat his presuppositions so he can hear how foolish they are
• Since their objection is going to be based upon subjective reasons, relate your questions to objective biblical reasons.
• Contrast its ultimate consequences (a consistent record of failure throughout history) with the historic record of success of communities, states and nations who have followed Christian principles.
• Explain which self-governing sphere(s) should be handling the issue (Individual, Family, Church, State).
• Present a humble, yet bold presentation of the Gospel

WEEK 51
Christians should not want to have anything to do with politics, or with reforming culture because politics is corrupted by sin!

This is a very curious objection. First, people say "Christians should have nothing to do with politics." Then they say "It is corrupt and is inhabited by untrustworthy people." The question that begs to be asked of such people is "What kind of behavior do you expect when the public square is left to non-Christians?" Since it is impossible to separate one's religion (ethics) from one's day-to-day decisions, shouldn't our concern be about "corrupting culture with righteousness," rather than letting non-Christians "corrupt culture by their unrighteous and sinful ethics?" Yes, "politics" is dirty, but so is business, law, education, sports and every other activity. It's part of the human condition known as sin. We've been called to be a leavening influence in our communities for holiness. We can't carry out our Calling by keeping God's wisdom inside our homes and Churches.

Non-Christians, who are so openly upset with the prospect of Christians becoming influential in civil government show their true colors of believing that in order for social change to take place, people must be coerced by external means (i.e., taxpayer funded public education, health and social services).

In direct opposition to this is the Christian view that societies are changed through inward regeneration, not outward revolution. (1 John 3.3; Colossians 1.13) Instead of top-down mandated change from a tyrannical central government, change comes from the bottom up, which means that it would take a substantial number of citizens living according to a Christian worldview for such change to take place.

We have no option but to interact with culture. For those who say they don't want to have anything to do with politics, you may want to give them this advice from the Greek philosopher Pericles, who writes, "Just because you don't take an interest in politics doesn't mean politics won't take an interest in you." Pericles wrote this 450 years before the birth of Christ!

> *The kingdoms of this world have become the kingdoms of our Lord and of His Christ and He shall reign forever and ever.*　　　REVELATION 11.15

> *I do not pray that You should take them out of the world, but that You should keep them from the evil one.*　　　JOHN 17.15

> *And Jesus came and spoke to them, saying, "All authority has been given to Me in heaven and on earth. Go therefore and make disciples of all the nations, baptizing them in the name of the Father and of the Son and of the Holy Spirit, teaching them to observe all things that I have commanded you; and lo, I am with you always, even to the end of the age." Amen.*　　　MATTHEW 28.18-20

IN YOUR OWN WORDS

Casting down arguments and every high thing that exalts itself against the knowledge of God, bringing every thought into captivity to the obedience of Christ.
2 CORINTHIANS 10.5

KeyPoints

_____

_____

_____

_____

_____

_____

_____

_____

_____

A Model for "Thawing the ICE" of a Non-Christian's Heart

Issue summarized
  Q. "What do you mean by that?"
  Q. "If that is the case, then what do you say about …?"
  Q. Point out the KeyPoints you listed in the above space.

Clarify the religion* associated with it (*worldview/philosophy)
  Q. "Upon what authority do you base your opinion?" (= "Why should I believe you?")
  Q. "Are you willing to base your eternal destiny upon your view?"

Expose it for the self-contradicting foolishness that it is.
• Repeat his presuppositions so he can hear how foolish they are
• Since their objection is going to be based upon subjective reasons, relate your questions to objective biblical reasons.
• Contrast its ultimate consequences (a consistent record of failure throughout history) with the historic record of success of communities, states and nations who have followed Christian principles.
• Explain which self-governing sphere(s) should be handling the issue (Individual, Family, Church, State).
• Present a humble, yet bold presentation of the Gospel

Don't you know that the idea of a Christian State is impossible, because the world is now under the dominion of Satan.

Such a defeatist attitude reflects a futuristic view of God's victorious promises, which makes our present actions and decisions meaningless. If such an interpretation of Scripture were accurate it would mean that God's Word would be reduced to "God loves you" with no explicit instructions on how to live and govern ourselves.

Satan's reign over the world began with the Fall of Man. While Satan is powerful, his control only extends over non-Christians. The apostle John teaches, "He who is in us is greater than he who is in the world." [1] The writer of Hebrews clarifies Satan's defeated state:

> *Since the children have flesh and blood, [Christ] too shared in their humanity*
> *so that by His death He might destroy him who holds the power of death –*
> *that is the devil – and free those who all their lives were held in slavery by*
> *their fear of death.*   HEBREWS 2.14-15

Satan will not be driven back by an instantaneous supernatural act of God, but rather by the obedience of Christians to God's commands and a faithful accepting of God's promises. In other words, our Calling is to complete the defeat of Satan.

A key question these objectors should answer is "Since Christ has been appointed 'head over all things to the church,' [2] why would it be imagined that His jurisdiction would include only individuals, and not also nations? And, since His authority does, indeed, extend over the nations, they must acknowledge Him as their sovereign authority. Christ has always raised up nations, or destroyed them, based upon their obedience or disobedience to His will. [3] Isaiah, in predicting the birth of our Lord, Savior, and King promises "the government will rest on [Christ's] shoulders." [4] A psalmist adds, "Blessed is the nation whose God is the Lord." [5] All of this goes to say that the nations are bound to recognize the Bible as the supreme law of the land; as the standard of civil legislation. Isaiah adds "The nation and the kingdom which will not serve You will perish." [6] When a godly king is commended, it is said "He clings to the Lord and departs not from His commandments," [7] and when an ungodly king is censured, he is accused of "not obeying the voice of the Lord." [8]

NOTES

1 1 John 4.4
2 Ephesians 1.22
3 Isaiah 43.3

4 Isaiah 9.6
5 Psalm 33.12
6 Isaiah 60.6-12

7 2 Kings 18.6
8 2 Kings 18.12

IN YOUR OWN WORDS

Casting down arguments and every high thing that exalts itself against the knowledge of God, bringing every thought into captivity to the obedience of Christ.   2 CORINTHIANS 10.5

KeyPoints

_____

_____

_____

_____

_____

_____

_____

_____

_____

A Model for "Thawing the ICE" of a Non-Christian's Heart

Issue summarized
  Q. "What do you mean by that?"
  Q. "If that is the case, then what do you say about …?"
  Q. Point out the KeyPoints you listed in the above space.

Clarify the religion* associated with it (*worldview/philosophy)
  Q. "Upon what authority do you base your opinion?" (= "Why should I believe you?")
  Q. "Are you willing to base your eternal destiny upon your view?"

Expose it for the self-contradicting foolishness that it is.
• Repeat his presuppositions so he can hear how foolish they are
• Since their objection is going to be based upon subjective reasons, relate your questions to objective biblical reasons.
• Contrast its ultimate consequences (a consistent record of failure throughout history) with the historic record of success of communities, states and nations who have followed Christian principles.
• Explain which self-governing sphere(s) should be handling the issue (Individual, Family, Church, State).
• Present a humble, yet bold presentation of the Gospel

WANT MORE DAILY READS?
ASK ABOUT VOLUMES 2 & 3

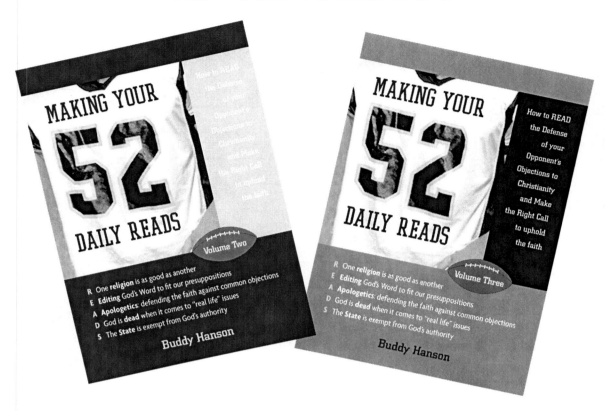

Some of the Volume 2 Issues

- "What can I do to improve my prayers?"
- "Why is it so important that I conform my business plan to God's Word?"
- "Can you imagine living in a 'Christianized' world?"
- "What are the four keys to cultural victory?"
- "What are six things a Christian can do to make his daily walk holier?"
- "Have you been too busy chopping wood to sharpen your Spiritual axe?"
- "What are the Ten Traits of Successful Leaders?"

Some of the Volume 3 Issues

- Satan's "Not So Sweet" Sixteen
- Seven Guidelines for members of Christ's Kingdom
- We must not forget who God is, who we are, and what we have been called to do
- We need to advance from a mere acknowledgment of biblical truths to an application of biblical truths
- All law is "religious"

APPENDIX ONE
Five Biblical Principles I May Encounter *Today*!

NON-CHRISTIANS OFTEN CITE THE ABILITY OF HUMANS TO COMMUNICATE TO all fellow humans, as well as our ability to make sophisticated decisions about how to live as the major differences between humans and animals. As usual, they are about half right. Since they don't believe in the soul and the supernatural, they leave those out of their equation. Putting aside the topics of the soul and the supernatural for another discussion, let's look at how we can easily improve our God-given ability to communicate with each other, as well as with our non-Christian neighbors.

The thought of presenting and/or defending Christian ideas to non-Christians is intimidating to many Christians. While we tend to get bogged down in our preparation of how to communicate God's true ideas, non-Christians are eager to engage us with the aberration of their false ideas. For the most part, we never think we're quite ready to confront them, while they prove that "ignorance is bliss" [1] by being eager to demonstrate their heady advantage over us. When you think about it (which is arguably the least thing that many Christians do), this is a remarkable situation. Those who have not been enlightened with God's wisdom are proclaiming that we who have been enlightened by Him are fools, and we in turn, live as though we are trying to prove their assessment of us correct by continuing to follow their rules! Even though we admit that Scripture refers to non-Christians as "fools," [2] we are the ones who are living foolishly because we approach each day as though we are mindless of the wisdom that God has graciously placed in our heart! Non-Christians can't help the fact that they are wisdomless. That's the way each of us comes into this world. It's only natural for them to hate God and to imagine that they are smarter and wiser than He is. We, however, have no excuse for being mindless of the wisdom He has given to us. We agree that we were once, "by nature children of wrath." We know that when we were "dead in our trespasses and sins," and willingly "walked according to the course of this world," that we were mercifully "made alive together with Christ." [3] As a result of these unspeakable mercies of God, we know that we now have a "living hope through the resurrection of Jesus Christ," [4] and that we have been "delivered from the power of the devil." [5] Yet, many of us continue to willingly, if grudgingly, consent to the cultural agenda of non-Christians! No wonder Jesus says that "the sons of this world are more shrewd in their generation than the sons of light."[6] Jesus' point is not that non-Christians are really wiser than we are, but that by our refusing to counter their unwise plans and schemes, we are allowing them to expand Satan's unholy influence throughout the earth, rather than our expanding Jesus' holy influence throughout the earth. In other words, culture doesn't operate in a vacuum. It will be directed according to the flow of either godly or ungodly ideas. Since our Creator God is in charge of His creation, He promises to bring blessings upon those who obey Him and curses upon those who disobey Him. [7]

Whether a person is a Christian or a non-Christian, the first thing to do before addressing any issue is to define the issue and then to determine what they want to accomplish. From the get-go we should have an overwhelming advantage in our discernment of the issues before us. This is so fundamental that it should go without saying, but sadly, our decisions rarely differ from the decisions non-Christians make, which results in our lifestyles mirroring theirs, instead of the other way around. So, let us remind ourselves that the first consideration of decision-making is:

 Do we want to make a decision to maintain the status-quo, or to un-quo the status?

In order to arrive at the correct perspective for this answer, the second consideration is:

 Are we interested in a possible (non-biblical) improvement, or an actual (biblical) improvement?

At this point, I would expect many readers to say: "Tell me something I don't know!" My response is: "Show me by your daily decisions that you believe what you know by practicing it." Since the "earth is the Lord's and the fullness thereof," [8] and we have been "adopted into God's family," [9] life's decision-making field is greatly tilted in our favor. But for the last century and a half we have given the "tilt" a "jilt" by refusing to factor God's inerrant counsel into our daily decision-making. We have rejected the objective answers of revelation, and relied upon the subjective answers of non-Christian speculation.

While we believe in an intentionally created *cause and effect* universe by a personal Creator God, we should (!) look to the lessons of history to guide our decisions. Non-Christians, on the other hand, who believe in an unintentional "Big Bang" beginning of the universe, have no absolute ethical standard upon which to base their decisions, so they are limited to a process of *flaws and correct*. They know that they don't have an absolute "divining rod," or "Rosetta Stone" to guide their decision-making, so they attempt to use their flawed thinking and reasoning as best they can, all the while knowing that they will have to make constant corrections to their decisions and plans. Since they reject a purposeful beginning to the earth and themselves, they know that they cannot expect a purposeful ending to their decisions or to life. This puts them in a condition whereby they are constantly *perceiving* the truth of man's word, while we (should be) constantly *receiving* the truth of God's Word.

We say that we don't like the direction in which our culture is going, but we refuse to do anything about it because we continue to refuse to conform our daily decisions to biblical truths. Since the opposite of *truth* is *lie*, this means we are living according to lies, which means that we are living according to Satan's agenda for the earth, instead of God's agenda.[10] Even though we adamantly profess to be Christians, we continue to live as though we did before our conversion, by feverishly attempting to keep our head above the steadily rising filthy waters of a non-Christian cultural agenda. In the words of the 20th century Southern philosopher, Richard Weaver, "We've raised 'muddling through' to the height of a science!" [11] Professor Weaver's point is that as people who have been called into Christ's most excellent Kingdom, there is no biblical reason for us to approach life with the mediocre attitude of merely "muddling through."

As we all would be quick to say, "Jesus has given us a perfect recipe for improving our culture." But in order for His recipe for living to produce the results we desire, we must use the most important ingredient of consistent and faithful obedience. In other words, simply *knowing* what his Word says, isn't enough. We must *do* it! As He explains to the Pharisees, "How can one enter a strong man's house and plunder His goods, unless he first binds the strong man?" [12] This remark to the Pharisees refers to the fact that Jesus bound Satan when he defeated his temptations in the wilderness. [13] And in order for us to "plunder his cultural agenda," we must conform our decisions (lifestyle) to Jesus' instructions. Once we begin to do that we will demonstrate to our non-Christian neighbors that we are "with Jesus," and He will reward our efforts by enabling us to "gather" them into His family and to live biblically-obedient lives! [14]

The following chart summarizes a few of the unassailable advantages we have over our non-Christian neighbors. Advantages that most of them don't realize we have, and don't realize that it is even possible to have, because we so rarely demonstrate them. May we be ashamed of such disobedience to our Lord, Savior and King, and of our distrust in His perfect will for how to live our lives. May we "repent, turn to God, and do works befitting repentance," [15] so that we won't "perish." [16]

Is Your Approach to Life Based Upon Certainty vs. Uncertainty?

NON-CHRISTIANS HAVE

- Man's traditions
- Abstract precedent opinion
- Relative prospective
- Speculation of current circumstances
- Continuous confusion
- Never-ending questions

CHRISTIANS HAVE

- God's definitions
- Concrete resident truth
- Absolute perspective

- Revelation from the triune God
- Constant clarity
- Always-comforting answers

When you base your decisions upon circumstances, at best, you can only expect your decision to "work" only as long as the current circumstances last!

The next time you are tempted to conclude that something in the news, whether it is a court decision, or a new legislative policy "just doesn't make sense," think about how that decision came to be. In all likelihood you will realize that we who have been given wisdom were mentally barricaded inside our homes and churches, while those who have no wisdom were directly involved in making that court decision or legislation. King Solomon warns of this very thing. Please give serious concentration to the counsel he quotes from Jehovah:

> *Because I have called and you refused, I have stretched out my hand and no one regarded, because you disdained all my counsel, and would have none of my rebuke, I also will laugh at your calamity; I will mock when your terror comes, when your terror comes like a storm, and your destruction comes like a whirlwind, when distress and anguish come upon you. Then they will call on me, but I will not answer; they will seek me diligently, but they will not find me. Because they hated knowledge and did not choose the fear of the LORD, they would have none of my counsel and despised my every rebuke. Therefore they shall eat the fruit of their own way, and be filled to the full with their own fancies. For the turning away of the simple will slay them, and the complacency of fools will destroy them; but whoever listens to me will dwell safely, and will be secure, without fear of evil."* PROVERBS 1.31-33

As Jonathan Edwards preaches, and as the Apostle Paul writes: "It is a fearful thing to fall into the hands of the living God." We like to think about how much God loves us, and that is most true, but it is equally true that our God is a just God and is "vengeful" against those who repeatedly disobey His perfect counsel. Listen to Paul's words to the Jewish Christians who were scattered outside of Palestine:

> *For we know Him who said, "Vengeance is Mine, I will repay," says the Lord. And again, "The LORD will judge His people." It is a fearful thing to fall into the hands of the living God.* HEBREWS 10.30-31

The Holy Spirit has mercifully replaced our original heart that was motivated toward sin, with a new spiritual heart that is motivated toward holiness. This enables us to "walk in God's statutes, keep His judgments, do them, and be His people." [17] This proclamation by the prophet Ezekiel, and repeated by Jeremiah [18] and the Apostle Paul, [19] is most significant because without the work of the Holy Spirit in our heart we would continue to live as a "brood of vipers" who speak evil things. [20] Jesus explains:

> *A good man out of the good treasure of his heart brings forth good things, and an evil man out of the evil treasure brings forth evil things. But I say to you that for every idle word men may speak, they will give account of it in the day of judgment.* MATTHEW 12.34-36

In Luke's account of this conversation, Jesus says, that the decisions we make and the words we speak come from our heart. Therefore, if we call Jesus "Lord," but continue to make our daily decisions according to our will, we are giving a strong indication that our heart has not been changed.

> *For every tree is known by its own fruit. For men do not gather figs from thorns, nor do they gather grapes from a bramble bush.*   LUKE 6.44-46

This is why King Solomon urges us to "Keep our heart with all diligence, for out of it spring the issues of life." [21] Paul adds that "God commanded light to shine" in our unconverted dark heart "to give us the light of knowledge of the glory of God." [22] This is why we, as Christians, have no option but to base every decision we make upon biblical truths. [23] We must not forget that every decision we make reflects the "god" that we trust, and not necessarily the "god" in which we profess to believe. Ultimately, we will demonstrate that the "god" of our decisions is either:

a. Peer pressure
b. Your family and/or tradition
c. Your boss
d. Current circumstances
e. The U.S. Supreme Court
f. Popular opinion
g. Abstract legal precedents
h. Concrete revelation from God

Someone may say, "Buddy, I know that as a Christian, I have the truth, and that my non-Christian neighbors don't have it. I also know that this gives me an insurmountable advantage over them since I can present God's holy and perfect wisdom, and all they have to counter it is their sinful and imperfect foolishness. However, I don't know how to begin the conversation because it seems to me that I would first need to have an encyclopedic knowledge to counter all of their objections!"

It is true that non-Christians have a seemingly never-ending list of objections to Christianity, and an equal amount of objections to our attempts to incorporate biblical reasons into our daily decision-making. As we have seen, however, the good news is that all of these possible objections can be easily grouped according to five categories under the acronym READS. Whether you are defending Christianity in principle, or defending the necessity to conform a decision to biblical truths, most of the objections you will encounter will fall under one of the following five categories:

- Faith vs. Reason   Jeremiah 17.9
- The universe is "random," not "orderly"   Genesis 1.1
- Miracles are impossible   Matthew 19.26
- Man's wisdom is sufficient   James 3.14-17
- Truth is "relative," not "absolute"   Proverbs 26.11-13

A biblical refutation for each of these objections is noted to help you in beginning to build your answer. Knowing that you have well thought out answers to these common objections will give you great confidence and should allow you to get your faithful testimony for God out of neutral and into high gear. In addition to these general tendencies, the READS acronym equips you with some specific tendencies of non-Christians by allowing you to quickly categorize a particular objection into one of five categories. In effect, we have reduced a seemingly infinite number of objections, down to five categories. Think you can handle that? I thought so. You've always known that you had God in your corner, and the READS acronym enables you to know how to get out of your corner and answer each day's "bell" as you exit your home for your vocation!

To review, the READS acronym stands for:

R   One **religion** is as good as another.
E   **Editing** God's Word to fit our presuppositions.
A   **Apologetics**; defending the faith against common objections by reducing their arguments to absurdity.
D   God is **dead** when it comes to "real life" issues.
S   The **State** is exempt from God's authority

R   One religion is as good as another.
This statement reflects two non-Christian presuppositions:

- Man's subjective relative *fiction* is better than God's objective absolute *truth*
- *Man's ethics* are better than *God's ethics*

Non-Christians make fun of us because we believe in absolute truth, [24] but in doing so they admit that all that's left for them to believe in is "fiction," because for them "truth" either doesn't exist, or it is relative to each person's beliefs. While their decisions are made with only their interests at heart, our decisions must be made to reflect the motivations of our new heart and God's interests. The primary question we must ask ourselves before making any decision is:

 Will this decision bring honor to God by conforming to a biblical truth? [25]

The primary concern of non-Christians is to bring honor to themselves, since they reject the biblical account of creation and a Creator God. For them, the "creation account" is a fairy tale, meant for earlier and less educated peoples, but in dismissing it, they also dismiss the possibility of objectively defining or defending how a person should live. They profess to live according to "science," while accusing us of living according to "faith," yet without a purposeful beginning of creation and humanity, *their system cannot function according to fixed rules of science, because they don't believe in any fixed rules!* The only way they can practice science, is to borrow our absolute principles, which they laughingly dismiss as superstitious, intolerant and unkind. The following question exposes the hypocrisy of their position:

We believe in science because we believe in a created and orderly universe, whereby the same actions will produce the same results. Since you don't believe in absolute truth, upon what basis do you base your scientific results?

Our "purposeful" beginning means we have absolute, objective and orderly principles upon which to base all of our decisions. Their "random" beginning provides no "purpose," and no definition of how they "ought" to live. Challenge them with these questions and then be quiet while they attempt to wiggle their way out of them:

You talk about various "facts," so explain to me how any "fact" could have a certain (absolute) meaning in an irrational universe that had a random (uncertain) beginning?

Since you don't believe in absolute truth, how does your worldview make sense of events and circumstances?

Since your worldview cannot account for "reason," or "logic," why are we even having this conversation?

The Self-Attesting Authority of Scripture

Because of the effects of Adam and Eve's disobedience on everyone's intellect we must depend solely upon Scripture to define correct ethical behavior (and to define God). Our "faith" is not like the blind leap evolutionists make, but is based upon "wisdom" [26] and "reason." [27] Our supernatural wisdom comes from God the Father and Jesus, [28] plus the Holy Spirit who writes God's law on our hearts at our conversion. Our commanded duty is to demonstrate this perfect way to live to our non-Christian neighbors. [29]

He has shown you, O man, what is good; and what does the LORD require of you but to do justly, to love mercy, and to walk humbly with your God?
                                                                    MICAH 6.8

You guide me with Your counsel and afterward receive me to glory.
                                                                    PSALM 73.24

All we can know of what we are — and what is good for us — is that we know nothing.
                                                                    SOCRATES

My belief in a Creator God who rules and overrules all events in His creation enables me to objectively know how to live, but since you believe in subjective truth (chance, luck, karma, etc.), how can you have confidence that what you know today will have any meaning tomorrow?

When a non-Christian claims that, "No one can prove that the Bible is absolutely true," he is placing man's logic and reason above that of the Triune God of Scripture! (even though his system of thinking and reasoning can't account for logic, since they only believe in what they can see, feel, and taste!) Therefore, their thinking that man's reason is ultimate is delusional!

> *For as the heavens are higher than the earth, so are ... My thoughts higher than your thoughts.*　　　　　　　　　　Isaiah 55.9

The epistemological* advantage we have over non-Christians is that by having God's Word as our final authority, *we don't have to know every fact exhaustively*, because God knows it. The non-Christian, on the other hand, *either has to know every fact*, or *be forced to admit that he is taking most of what he believes on faith*! In other words, it is impossible for him to prove what he believes!

Non-Christians admit that they live in a chaotic universe, surrounded by isolated "facts" that have no meaning other than what any particular generation randomly attaches to them. Such a definition of reality means that non-Christians cannot point to any particular set of ethics as the best way to live. For them, history is meaningless as they can only conclude that some generations and societies have been "luckier" than others. In contrast to the fuzzy "wishes" of non-Christians who hope they can figure out the best way to live and raise their families, the prophet Isaiah provides some specificsfor both Israel and Judah to "Keep justice, and do righteousness." [30] Approximately one hundred years later Jehovah included additional specifics on how to carry out His will on earth: "Do no wrong and do no violence to the stranger, the fatherless, or the widow, nor shed innocent blood in this place." [31]

Will this decision assist me (us) in "doing no wrong and in doing no violence to the stranger, the fatherless, or the widow, nor shed innocent blood? [32]

It is most important for us to recognize that when we see the injunctions to be merciful and to treat our neighbors with justice, the only acceptable definitions for these behaviors must come from God's revealed Word. The Ten Commandments provide God's skeletal definition of how we are supposed to live (commandments 5-10), as well as the authority behind our ethics (commandments 1-4). [33]

---

* Epistemology – How we know what we know.

? *Since your worldview positions you as a product of primordial slime, how can you know for certain what "good," and/or "evil" behavior is?*

? *I have the self-attesting Word of God to enable me to define human dignity, science and morality, how does your worldview enable you to define these issues?*

E   Editing God's Word to fit our presuppositions.

As King David thought about the marvelous creation that God had brought into existence, he records his thoughts of amazement that we were made to have dominion over it.

> *When I consider Your heavens, the work of Your fingers, the moon and the stars, which You have ordained, what is man that You are mindful of him, and the son of man that You visit him? For You have made him a little lower than the angels, and You have crowned him with glory and honor. You have made him to have dominion over the works of Your hands; You have put all things under his feet.*   PSALM 8.3-6

Another psalmist exclaims, "The heaven, even the heavens, are the LORD's; *but the earth He has given to the children of men.*" [34] Certainly, it should be clear that we are not only "winners" in eternity, but also right here on earth! When non-Christians call us "foolish, backward, and superstitious" it is the "pot" that is calling the "kettle" black. All-in-all non-Christians have

- no way to differentiate themselves from animals
- no way to determine what their life's purpose is, and
- no predictable hope for the future
- no explanation of why they are living here instead of another planet
- no timeless truths to live by, and/or to pass on to their children, or others
- no defense for what they believe, including no way to definitively disprove anyone who disagrees with them (since in their view there are no "absolute" answers!)

These six items clearly reveal that non-Christians don't have a lot going for them. When turned into questions, they would parallel the six questions all aspiring journalism students are taught to answer in writing news stories. The same questions also need to be answered in writing our life's story. As the following chart illustrates, only Christians are able to answer them, which means that only Christians are able to "write" a meaningful life story! The questions are listed in the same order as the above six items.

Our belief in absolute truth and an orderly and created universe means that we can conduct scientific experiments, and change the variables to find out which brings about the best results. We also have the confidence that the results we receive from one experiment will be the same for all future experiments as long as we use the same formula. Non-Christians can never be certain of this, because of their disbelief in absolute truth. They can't even account for why a particular experiment produced the results it did!

The Six Unanswerable Questions for Non-Christians

QUESTION	CHRISTIAN	NON-CHRISTIAN
Who?	Creature of God	No Idea
What?	Undeserving Ambassador of God who has been called out of darkness and "into light" through God's merciful grace.	No Idea
When?	God will bless our obedience in His perfect timing to a "thousand generations."	No Idea
Where?	We're living in God's creation on our way to Heaven, encouraging those on their way to Hell to repent and join us.	No Idea
Why?	Carry out God's will on earth so that the earth will be full of the knowledge of the LORD as the waters cover the sea.	No Idea
How?	Present a godly lifestyle (testimony) for our non-Christian neighbors to observe, share the Gospel, and teach God's principles for living to our families and others.	No Idea

---

 Does this decision indicate that I am "departing from iniquity," or taking part in iniquity? [35]

A Apologetics; defending the faith against common objections by reducing their arguments to absurdity.

Peter tells us to "always be ready" to present and defend the faith.

But sanctify the Lord God in your hearts, and always be ready to give a defense to everyone who asks you a reason for the hope that is in you, with meekness and fear; having a good conscience, that when they defame you as evildoers, those who revile your good conduct in Christ may be ashamed. For it is better, if it is the will of God, to suffer for doing good than for doing evil.

1 PETER 3.15-17

Paul adds to Peter's advice by instructing us to avoid foolish and undisciplined questions. The first way to do this is to ask them what authority their opinions are based upon. Even though a non-Christian may be very intelligent, it is impossible for him to reason logically because they are not basing their thoughts on God's absolute truth. Don't let them forget that they love to state: "If something cannot be seen, felt, touched, smelled or tasted, it doesn't exist." They may not have noticed in their "futile" or "vain" mind, [36] to use Paul's words, but *"logic" is not a physical thing!* So they continue to "profess to be wise, but become fools" instead. [37] In God's eyes, their communication is "profane and idle babbling." [38]

Show Them the Foolishness Of Their Wisdom

Our main objective when confronted by a non-Christian, is to show them, in a nice and compassionate way, the foolishness of their reasoning. So, rather than being intimidated at what may at first appear to be a very formidable objection, you need only keep the objector talking. By doing this you will discover the basic presuppositions that they take for granted in their reasoning. Even though non-Christians will initiate the conversation regarding their questions about Christianity, it is not God who is on trial. Quite the opposite, *it is they who are on trial and who need to present their defense.* Their minds are "at war" with God [39] and it is we who can help them see this as we get them to hear themselves explain their concerns. In the words of Dr. Greg Bahnsen, we must "reduce the non-Christian's arguments to absurdity." [40] Paul and James say that our first principle is to:

Avoid foolish and undisciplined questions knowing that they produce quarrels, and a servant of the Lord must not quarrel, but must be gentle toward all, skillful in teaching, patient, one who courteously instructs those who oppose themselves, if perhaps God may grant to them conversion unto a genuine knowledge of truth.   2 TIMOTHY 2.23-25; JAMES 3.13-17

It can usually be determined if the objector is sincere, or is simply attempting to goad us into an argument. Once we determine that an objector is not serious, the best course of action is to break off the conversation. Courteously make a statement, such as: "I believe that the triune God in Scripture exists. You say that you don't believe it, but I know that in your heart you do know He exists. [41] So, if you ever want to have a serious conversation about God, I'll be happy to talk with you."

Our second and third principles come from Proverbs 26.4-5:

Do not answer a fool according to his folly, lest you also be like him; answer a fool according to his folly lest he be wise in his own eyes.

What is King Solomon asking us to do here? First, he tells us not to answer a fool "according to his folly" so that we won't be like him. Then he tells us to answer a fool "according to his folly" so he won't be wise in his own eyes! At first glance it sounds like Solomon is talking in a circle. This is what he means:

We should carefully listen to the objector because in presenting to us the reasons why he believes, he will be giving us ammunition for us to use in questioning him about his beliefs.

If you answer a non-Christian's objection without having him fully explain it, you will be adding validity to his position. However, by keeping him talking, you will unlevel the playing field between him and you, and, as mentioned, *the field is definitely not level!* Since "the field" belongs to God, [42] you always have Home Field Advantage! You have the benefits of supernatural truth and wisdom, while the objector has the disadvantages of natural foolishness and fiction. The only thing is *he doesn't realize that his reasoning is foolish, and unless and until we show him that such is the case, he's not going to be interested in our answer.* Think about it like this: Your purpose is to move the conversation from debating your positions, to having the non-Christian defend his position. Or, to look at it another way: to move the discussion from the objector putting God on trial, to your putting him and his beliefs on trial. Your first question could be:

 Upon what "authority" do you base your opinion?

In other words, how does he know that his ethical standard is the correct standard? If he can't point to an absolute standard (which he can't), this means that his worldview is based upon subjectivity. Explain that this puts him at a distinct disadvantage in discussing anything with you, because your worldview is based upon the absolute truths of the Bible, which means that you can prove your arguments, but he can't.

The key is to keep the non-Christian talking and explaining his why he believes what he believes until he says something that contradicts his worldview (which, sooner or later, he will, since his entire worldview is based upon contradictions). For example, if he exclaims, "I believe in 'reason,' whereas you believe in 'faith.'" As discussed, ask him how his worldview would allow him to believe in "reason," since he only believes in things that can be seen, touched, smelled or tasted. Ask him, "Have you *seen reason*? Have you *touched*, or *smelled*, or *tasted* it?"

If you are concerned that you know little, if anything, about various false religions, don't be. The only phrase you need to use to keep the non-Christian talking until he contradicts his worldview is: *If that is the case, then what do you say about …?* (and then repeat back to him what he has just said, and wait for him to respond. After he responds, or if he doesn't respond, say, "I'm sorry to have interrupted you, please continue.") By following this procedure you are not giving credibility to his objection, and so are not becoming "like him" (second principle). And, as you continue to ask questions based upon his answers you will be letting him hear (in his own words!) *the foolishness of his objection* (third principle), so that he is no longer "wise in his own eyes." [43] In this way *the non-Christian winds up opposing himself,* by his own foolish presuppositions.

The fourth principle, in approaching your apologetic duty, is to switch his thinking over to "objective" parameters. Since you have the truth, there is no reason for you to go outside of Scripture in order to attempt to "build a bridge" for your conversation with him. After all,

> *It is the objective absolute truth of God's Word that gives you an insurmountable advantage over the subjective relative truth of the non-Christian.*

Remember, this is your Home Field advantage, so the last thing you want to do is to "play" on his field, because his field only allows subjective and emotional "feelings." God's field, on the contrary, contains the Creator God's truth [44] to which we creatures must conform if we have any hope of overcoming the non-Christian cultural agenda and of coming to the correct decisions in our homes, churches and vocations. Therefore,

> *Any attempt to create a "common ground rapport" with a non-Christian outside of God's Word will be an attempt to use "untruthful methods" in order to inform him of the truth! Why should you expect such a tactic to work?*

Your calling is to help the non-Christian clearly see that his worldview is based upon sand. [45] As Dr. Cornelius Van Til states: "It's not about winning. It's about exposing their inconsistency. God does everything else. Never forget the antithesis." [46] Once the Holy Spirit changes his heart so that he can recognize the truth, he will see how hopeless his condition and worldview is, and will be motivated to repent and turn his life over to Jesus.

The fifth principle to use in your conversations with non-Christians is to present a humble, yet bold presentation of the Gospel. As mentioned, it is only after a person comes to the realization that his presuppositions about life are "foolish" that he will be interested in hearing the Gospel. We know that for the non-Christian to operate in the world and for any portion of his worldview to work, he must borrow Christian truths. The important point is the non-Christian doesn't realize this! Since he has tossed the principles of absolute, objective truth out of his philosophical window, he can't make sense of his value judgments! By his own admission "truth" either doesn't exist, or is relative to each person's opinions, which is the same as saying, "I realize that what I am saying makes no sense to you or anyone else, but it does to me!" As you find out which truths he is borrowing (by listening carefully to why he believes what he believes), you can use those to begin your conversation with him. From there you should point out the true context of the non-Christian's borrowed truth. So, no matter how smart or savvy he might appear, your approach in defending the faith is very simple.

The Five Steps of Apologetics

STEP ONE   Avoid questions that are designed to draw you into an argument.

STEP TWO   Repeat his presuppositions so he can hear how foolish they are.

STEP THREE   Carefully listen to the objection so you can question the basis of his beliefs (upon what authority are they based?).

STEP FOUR   Frame your answers according to objective biblical principles (which should demonstrate that God's Word is superior his subjective words).

STEP FIVE   Provide a humble yet bold presentation of the Gospel.

An example of a way that you can be on the offensive could go like this: "*OK, let's just for argument's sake, say...*" Then demonstrate the foolishness of his position by showing him the thought-through consequences of what he has just said, thereby reducing his position (worldview) to absurdity.

> *The proof of Christianity is the impossibility of the contrary.*[47]

The non-Christian's thinking must be completely turned around [48] so that he can see that for him to make sense of life, he must trust in the triune God of Scripture. As long as a person trusts in himself he will remain separated from the Lord. [49] As King Solomon writes, we must "Trust in the Lord with all our heart, and lean not upon our own understanding." [50]

Let the wicked forsake his way, and the unrighteous man his thoughts: and let him return unto the Lord. ISAIAH 55.7; COLOSSIANS 3.10

Show Non-Christians that they don't have an "ought"

One of the quickest ways to get the non-Christian to "fish or cut bait," in their conversation with you is to ask:

What is your "ultimate reference point" when it comes to deciding the correct course of action to take?

For non-Christians, they are their "ultimate reference point," whereas God is our "ultimate reference point." Instead of depending upon the never-changing *objective* truth of Scripture as their "reference point," non-Christians rely upon the ever-changing *subjective* imaginings of their conscience in attempting to be an original interpreter of reality. Our belief in God's absolute counsel enables us to discuss and debate the issues of the day within the context of how things "ought" to be. This gives us concrete guidelines for identifying why certain issues are going badly, and what we must do to correct them. Non-Christians, on the other hand, have no way of determining for certain the way we "ought" to live, since for them "truth" (if it exists) is left up to everyone's interpretation. [51] While we have "proof," they have "spoof." Their ideas are based upon "sand." [52] It must be frustrating to them that, regardless of how passionately they hold to a particular idea, that they can neither prove to us that it is right, or that biblical ideas are wrong!

According to the non-Christian mindset, "Evil has not come into the world because of man's disobedience; it is a metaphysical fact, it just is!" [53] We know, however, that it is only in God's light that we see light. [54] In other words, we are to think His thoughts after Him. Non-Christians, on their own, cannot "see the Light" [55] because the Holy Spirit has not given them a new spiritual heart and so they refuse to repent and place their faith in Jesus, who says: "*I* am the way, the truth and the life." [56] To the non-Christian way of thinking, this statement refers to them! To their way of thinking, *they* are "the way and the truth!"

Apologetics Confidence Builders

- Non-Christians can know things, but they cannot justify their knowledge of them.
- The best proof of God's existence is that without Him they can't prove anything.
- Don't let them "beg the question" (by assuming what they are trying to prove). Ask them to explain what they are taking for granted in their objections/beliefs.
- Ask why they believe what they do (how can they make sense of their argument without "borrowing Christian presuppositions."

"You're appealing to the very thing against which you are arguing!"
"If you really believe what you say, you can't say _____.")
"How did you come to hold that view?"
"How can you be certain that what you say you believe is true?
"Then ask them to define "truth."

Three Tried & True Principles

American Vision President Gary DeMar offers three guidelines for apologetics:

1. Refer the non-Christian to Scripture and never accept his authority.
2. Show him he also has an ultimate authority.
3. Demonstrate the superiority of Scripture to his authority. [57]

When working with other Christians on a particular cultural issue, you will have excellent opportunities to not only clear up some fuzzy thinking by fellow Christians by asking:

? *Will this decision help us to perpetuate a cultural ill (by dealing with a symptom), or will it help to obliterate a cultural ill (by dealing with the root cause)?* [58]

Often the proposed solutions will be more "conservative" than Christian and will give you an opening to evangelize those who are merely moralistic conservatives by asking:

? *Are we "tilting at windmills," by acting on man's thoughts, rather than "wilting Satan's plans" by acting on God's thoughts?* [59]

Another way to phrase the question is:

? *Are we basing our decision upon the ever-changing sand of man-made circumstances, or upon the never-changing solid rock of God-commanded truth?* [60]

Christians who suggest compromising an absolute principle of Christianity in the hope of gaining non-Christian support probably don't realize that by suggesting such a strategy or tactic, that they are placing current *circumstances* above *God's Word*. Put another way, they are placing *their wisdom* above *God's wisdom*. But while your questions are aimed at starting a discussion among Christians, the conservative moralists in the room will be able to hear some excellent reasons why Christianity is more than a profession of faith, and is, indeed, a way of life. Point this out by asking:

? *Does living out of conformity with the Word of God result in individuals and nations experiencing strife and turmoil?* [61]

When they answer, "Yes," say, "If we're serious about bringing about a successful solution to this issue, is there any biblical support to base our decision upon any counsel except God's Word? Unfortunately, it has been because Christians have not been faithful to ask this question before embarking upon a "cure" for a particular cultural ill, that we are now "sowing the seeds of what we've reaped." [62]

D God is dead when it comes to "real life" issues.

Nothing could be more untrue than this presupposition! God's Word not only tells us how the heavens and earth were created, but also describes our purpose for living, plus the ethics we should employ. Jesus chose His last recorded prayer to ask His Father to protect us from Satan [63] to give us time to "repair the ruins" of civilization. [64]

The first chapter of the first book of the Bible explains that we were created in God's image to "fill the earth and subdue it."

> *So God created man in His own image; in the image of God He created him;*
> *male and female He created them. Then God blessed them, and God said to*
> *them, "Be fruitful and multiply; fill the earth and subdue it; have dominion over*
> *the fish of the sea, over the birds of the air, and over every living thing that*
> *moves on the earth."*   GENESIS 1.27-28

Two chapters later, immediately after Adam and Eve's disobedience, Jehovah presents the first gospel sermon to them (and us!):

> *So the LORD God said to the serpent: "Because you have done this, you are*
> *cursed more than all cattle, and more than every beast of the field; on your belly*
> *you shall go, and you shall eat dust all the days of your life. And I will put*
> *enmity between you and the woman, and between your seed and her Seed; He*
> *shall bruise your head, and you shall bruise His heel."*   GENESIS 3.14-15

Non-Christians may think us a *fool*, but as these verses explain, we have been created to *rule*! Throughout the course of history Satan will deliver a painful blow to our heal, but we, through our faithful and consistent obedience, will deliver a fatal blow to his head! That doesn't sound very much like "God is dead to real life issues" to me! Cut to the chase with non-Christians, by asking:

? *God's Word clearly explains what He expects of our lifestyle. Upon what*
       authority do you base your worldview and lifestyle?

? *My belief in a Creator God who rules and overrules all events in His creation*
       enables me to objectively know how to live, but since you believe in subjective
       truth (chance, luck, etc.), how can you have confidence that what you know
       today will have any meaning tomorrow? [65]

Earlier we discussed various questions to ask when in a group that contained both Christians and non-Christians regarding cultural strategies and tactics. In those circumstances, when a person who professes to be a Christian says that we need to "take action" with regard to a certain cultural issue, ask him:

? *Do you believe that God's Word is absolutely true?*

If he answers "No," explain that they have no way of reaching an absolute answer, and are wasting his (and your) time discussing it. If the answer is "Yes," ask

? *Which of the Ten Commandments relates to this issue?*

If he says, "I'm not certain where in the Bible to find the biblical principle to follow," ask him to do some research and get back with you. If he is serious about his profession and the issue, he will try to find the biblical answer, and will either get back to you with it, or tell you that he can't find it. In this case, help him to find it, because he has demonstrated that he really wants to follow God's will. If he provides a particular commandment of God as the basis for his "solution" to the cultural issue, ask

? *What principle(s) does this commandment teach that helps us to build a God-honoring solution?*

Then discuss various strategies and tactics by which the cultural issue can be addressed. When a Christian proposes a "solution" to a cultural issue, ask

? *How did you arrive at that strategy/tactic/solution? Or*

? *Why are you confident that this strategy/tactic/solution will work? (What's the Biblical reason behind your idea?)*

If the proposed solution does not conform to Scripture, ask: "Should we do this and sin against the Lord?" [66]

? *If he says, "We'll get nowhere dealing with this issue strictly according to Scripture, we'll have to seek a middle ground approach." Ask, "Is there any point at which you place a "cap" on God's sovereignty? (i.e., what we, as Christians can accomplish through faithful, consistent obedience?) If this doesn't convict him to incorporate his biblical beliefs into his everyday decision-making, ask, "Is anything too hard for the LORD?"* [67]

When it comes to educating children, there is once again an insurmountable epistemological chasm that is impossible to cross for non-Christians. We have education in the *truth*, while they have whatever *propaganda* the "elite" that controls the civil government schools forces upon the students. This means that, since God never changes [68] His perfect counsel on how we should live remains the same throughout the years. We, as Christian parents, can confidently teach our children the correct way to live today, knowing that biblical truths will never go out of date.

Non-Christian parents, however, because of their belief in the ever-changing whims of public opinion, can have no confidence that the "accepted way" to raise their children today will be the same in years to come.

S   The *State* is exempt from God's authority.

While non-Christians favor a tyrannical top-down *central* civil government, Christians see in God's Word that His appointed method of governing comprises four *self-governing* spheres of the individual, family, church and state. Each sphere has its own set of specific accountabilities and is not to usurp the responsibilities of either of the other spheres. The factor unifying each of these four separate self-governing spheres is that each rules in accordance with biblical truths.

Our biblically-based capitalistic standards have a proven record throughout history of producing successful cultures that include an affluent middle class of citizens, with many personal liberties. Non-Christian civil governments have practically no personal liberties, which means that there is no motivation to improve one's condition. The predictable result of this is that there is no middle class, lots of poverty and a proven record of failure of all non-Christian civilizations throughout history.

Since we believe that people are special creations of God, we respect the life of males and females, adults and children. By believing in "objective truths," we can make and enforce civil laws to "keep the peace." Non-Christians, however, have no such concerns for the welfare of fellow humans, because of their belief that we're all nothing more than highly evolved tad poles.

This is why the Christianized Western civilization originated hospitals, adoption agencies, made possible social lives for women, established copyright laws, and written law codes, juries by peers, respect for those in authority, honor for parents, etc., etc., etc.

?   *Does this particular program being considered for legislation by the state conform to its biblically mandated accountabilities of protecting against a military invasion, and keeping our community safe?* [69]

?   *Will this decision result in civil rulers usurping one of the four God-appointed, self-governing spheres of the individual, family, state, and church?* [70]

NOTES

1 Shakespeare, William, *Winter's Tale*, A.2, S.1
2 Proverbs 1.7; Ephesians 5.15
3 Ephesians 2.1-5
4 1 Peter 1.3
5 Hebrews 2.14-15
6 Luke 16.8
7 Leviticus 26; Deuteronomy 28
8 Psalm 24.1
9 Ephesians 1.4-6
10 John 8.44-46
11 Weaver, Richard, *The Ethics of Rhetoric*, (Hermagoras Press, 1985), p. 83
12 Matthew 12.29
13 Matthew 4.1-11
14 Matthew 12.20
15 Acts 26.20
16 Luke 13.3-6
17 Ezekiel 11.19-20; 36.25-27
18 Jeremiah 31.33
19 Hebrews 8.9-10
20 Matthew 12.34
21 Proverbs 4.23
22 2 Corinthians 4.6-7
23 Romans 12.1-2
24 John 17.17; Psalm 119.142, 151
25 1 Corinthians 10.31
26 Job 38.36; James 1.5; 2 Timothy 3.15
27 Mark 12.30; Proverbs 3.7; 9.10
28 Colossians 2.2-3
29 Matthew 5.13-16
30 Isaiah 56.1
31 Jeremiah 22.3
32 Exodus 22.21-24
33 Exodus 20.1-17; Deuteronomy 5.6-21
34 Psalm 115.16
35 2 Timothy 2.19
36 Ephesians 4.17-19
37 Romans 1.22
38 1 Timothy 6.20
39 Romans 8.7
40 Bahnsen, Greg, *Pushing the Antithesis: The Apologetic Methodology of Greg L. Bahnsen*, Gary DeMar, Editor, (American Vision Press, 2007), p.146
41 Romans 1.18-23
42 Psalm 24.1
43 1 Peter 3.15
44 Psalm 119.160
45 Matthew 7.24-26
46 Bahnsen, DeMar, *ibid.*, *Pushing*, p. ix
47 Bahnsen, Dr. Greg, *Always Ready: Directions For Defending The Faith*, (Bahnsen, 1996), The Southern California Center for Christian Studies offers mini courses in Apologetics, Theonomic Ethics, Theology, and Political Ethics as well as seminary courses by correspondence. www.scccs.org
48 Ephesians 4.23-24
49 Jeremiah 17.5
50 Proverbs 3.5
51 1 Corinthians 1.20
52 Matthew 7.24-27
53 Van Til, Dr. Cornelius, *A Survey of Christian Epistemology*, den Delk Foundation, 1969
54 Psalm 36.9; 119.105
55 1 Corinthians 1.21
56 John 14.6
57 DeMar, Gary, *Thinking Straight in a Crooked World*, (AV Press, Powder Sptings, GA 2001), p.124; www.americanvision.org
58 Acts 5.39
59 Matthew 4.4
60 Romans 4.20-21
61 Leviticus 26; Deuteronomy 28
62 Hosea 8.7; Galatians 6.7
63 John 17.15
64 Ezra 9.9; Isaiah 61.4; Amos 9.11
65 Daniel 5.21
66 Genesis 39.9
67 Genesis 18.14
68 Numbers 23.19
69 Romans 13.1-7
70 Matthew 22.21

APPENDIX TWO
Daily Spiritual Practice

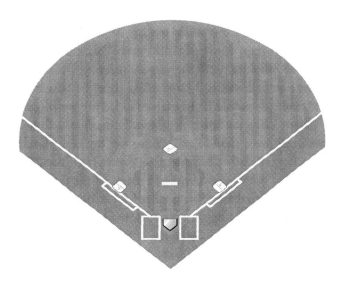

THE NEXT TIME YOU GO TO A BASEBALL GAME, MAKE CERTAIN THAT YOU GET settled in your seat at least 30 minutes before the game starts. Then pay particular attention to one of the most practical training methods of any vocation. It's called pre-game infield and outfield practice. In the brief span of about 10 minutes you will witness a coach with a long, skinny bat methodically take his players through the basic plays they will probably have to make during the game. He will begin by hitting a fly ball to each outfielder (so they can check the location of the sun, or lights, and any effect the wind may have on the ball), then he will hit a ground ball to them (so they can see how quickly, or slowly the ball gets to them so they will know whether to charge in on a hit, or wait and field it on a good hop). The outfielders will, in turn, make throws to the different bases, with the infielders lining up the throws to possibly cut them off, if necessary.

Then the coach will hit ground balls to each infielder. Notice how he will hit one ball right at them, one to their left, and one to their right. He will also mix-in hard hit balls and soft hit balls. The infielders will begin by throwing to first base, then they will throw to second base to complete a double play. Finally, the coach will hit a high pop up for the catcher, so he, like the outfielders, can get a feel for the sun, lights, and/or the wind effect.

A casual observer may think that this is simply some sort of traditional activity to warm-up the players, but as we've just seen, it is something far different. It is a **compact, succinct and comprehensive review of the basic plays that will probably have to be made in the game,** and it is done so quickly that the players don't have time to think about what to do, or where to position themselves on the field for a throw from the outfield. They simply react to the ball as it is hit by the coach.

The beauty of this brief practice exercise before each game is that it reinforces a critical skill that is necessary in winning: making the proper reaction. Once the ball is hit to a player there is no time to think about what to do with it. The player must have already rehearsed that decision *before* the play in case the ball is hit to him. This is why the pregame infield and outfield practice proceeds almost as though it were a choreographed dance. There are never any instructions yelled out by the coach. All of that has been taken care of in practice. On game day, he simply hits one ball after another from outfielder to outfielder, and infielder to infielder, with the players reacting with precision.

As a former college baseball coach, I have often thought how effective a 10-minute review of biblical fundamentals would be to each of us before we stepped from our homes each day. As we all know, once we leave the friendly confines of our homes, and go to work, or to school, we don't have time to call a time-out to think about how we are going to react to the constant flow of daily decisions. The fast pace of the 21st century demands that we react, in much the same way as an athlete reacts to the fast-changing situation on the ball field. This is not to say that there is no value in thinking through our decisions, but rather that the thinking and evaluating process of how to react in a certain situation must take place in our homes before we begin each day's "game."

The sheet on the following page is designed for you to use for your "Daily Spiritual Practice" before you leave home each day. It prepares you to make God-honoring decisions (1 Corinthians 10.31) by grouping the various topics you are likely to encounter into the five principles in the READS acronym. So, instead of *physically* fielding grounders or fly balls, and throwing to the proper base, or instead of throwing across the diamond to first base, or to second for a double play, make it a habit to *mentally* review these possible responses to the very probable questions and concerns you will encounter each day.

FIVE BIBLICAL PRINCIPLES I MAY ENCOUNTER TODAY!

Remember that your daily decisions reflect the "god" in which you trust, not necessarily the "god" in which you profess to believe. Ultimately, we will demonstrate that our "god" is either:

d.	Peer pressure	e.	The U.S. Supreme Court
e.	Your family and/or tradition	f.	Popular opinion
f.	Your boss	g.	Abstract legal precedent
g.	Current circumstances	h.	Concrete biblical truth

As a Christian, you have no option but to base every decision you make upon biblical truths. ROMANS 12.1-2; 1 CORINTHIANS 10.31

R One *religion* is as good as another.
- How will this decision help us to "crush Satan's head?" GENESIS 3.14-15
- Does this decision indicate we "have no hope and are without God in the world?" EPHESIANS 2.12
    PRINCIPLE: God, not Satan, rules the earth.

E *Editing* God's Word to fit our presuppositions, instead of establishing its ethics in our daily behavior.
- Does this decision indicate that I am "departing from iniquity," or taking part in iniquity? 2 TIMOTHY 2.19
- Does this decision "grieve the Holy Spirit" because it doesn't conform to biblical truths? EPHESIANS 4.30
    PRINCIPLE: The times are abnormal; we've been called to normalize them.

A *Apologetics*: defending the faith against common objections by reducing their arguments to absurdity.
- Will this decision help to perpetuate a cultural ill (by dealing with a symptom), or will it help to obliterate a cultural ill (by dealing with the root cause)? ACTS 5.39
- Am I "tilting at man's windmills," by acting on man's thoughts, rather than "wilting Satan's plans" by acting on God's thoughts? MATTHEW 4.4
    PRINCIPLE: We live in a universe, not a biverse (no "real life" and "religious" realms).

D God is *dead* when it comes to "real life" issues.
- Am I basing my decision upon the ever-changing subjective sand of man-made circumstances, or upon the never-changing objective solid rock of God-commanded truth? ROMANS 4.20-21
    PRINCIPLE: God is smarter and wiser than man.

S The *State* is exempt from God's authority.

- Will this decision result in civil rulers usurping one of the four God-appointed, self-governing spheres of the individual, family, state, and church? Matthew 22.21
- Does this proposed legislation conform to its limited biblically mandated accountabilities of protecting against a military invasion, and keeping our community safe? Or, is it proposing to spend our way out of a cultural issue (through higher taxes), instead of living our way our of it (by conforming our life style to biblical truths?) ROMANS 13.1-7

    PRINCIPLE: God created a cause-and-effect universe; not a random one.

Appendix Three
Presenting the Gospel

FOLLOWING ARE A COUPLE OF WAYS TO BRIDGE FROM A CONVERSATION INTO A brief presentation of the Gospel.

1. "What you've said interests me. I've found that many people have bits and pieces of religious knowledge but no clear and concise understanding of the theme of the Bible. Several people have found it helpful to hear a brief summary of this theme. I'm prepared to take 10 minutes to go over it with you right now. Could we do that? I really think you'd find it helpful." Or,
2. "What you've just said interests me. I'd like to know more about why you think that way. I wonder if you've ever considered this as an answer (or alternate view) to the point you just made..."

The Gospel (Ephesians 2.1-10)

Grace
1. Heaven is a free gift.
2. It is not earned or deserved.

Man
1. Is a sinner.
2. Cannot save himself.

God
1. Is merciful – He provides atonement for our sins if we repent.
2. Is just – He must punish sin.

Christ
1. Who He is – the infinite God-man.
2. What He did – paid for our sins and purchased a place in heaven which He gives as a gift to His elect.

Repentance and Faith

1. Repentance – being willing to turn from our sins.
2. Faith – What it is not—mere intellectual assent or temporal faith.
3. Faith – What it is—trusting Jesus Christ alone for salvation.

Points to include in our testimony

1. God is totally *just*. He rewards good and punishes evil (i.e. God, Obey).
2. We were originally made for *His purpose* and to be in *fellowship* with Him (i.e. Serve) but we rejected this offer. Non-Christians are now *separated* from God and must pay the price of sin. (i.e. Man)
3. God has *provided* a way of reconciliation. His *gift* is eternal life. (i.e. Christ)
4. The non-Christian *must admit* that he is a sinner, *confess* that Christ is his only answer and *accept* Him as both Lord and Savior. (i.e. Repent, Faith)
5. Christian faith is not a blind "leap in the dark." It is founded on more solid content than any other system of beliefs.

Phrasing our response

In our response we should quote what the other person has said, "You say that you know people are significant, and you need a system that says so ..."

> Must I make a public profession?" —Jesus teaches, "Everyone who shall confess Me before men, I will also confess before My Father who is in heaven. But whoever shall deny Me before men, I will also deny him before My Father.
>
> MATTHEW 10-32-33

Post-Gospel Presentation

- "Have you ever considered yourself a sinner according to the biblical definition?"
- "What do you think of what Jesus has done for sinners?"
- "What do you think of such a God who is a Creator and Redeemer?"
- "Is there any reason why you couldn't become a Christian?"

Repentance

God commands that fallen mankind repent (turn from our sins to Him, and begin living by His rules, instead of by our rules). He even causes His elect to repent (Acts 5.31; 11.18; 26.20; 2 Timothy 2.25-26).

The Relationship of	Faith and	Repentance
1. Great commission	Mark 16.16	Luke 24.46-47
2. What must be done to be saved	Acts 16.31	Acts 2.38
3. What Jesus taught	John 3.16	Luke 13.3-5
4. Both are of God's grace to the Jews	Acts 18.24-28	Acts 5.31
5. Both are of God's grace to the Gentiles	Acts 13.48	Acts 11.18

BIBLIOGRAPHY

Bahnsen, Greg
Always Ready: Directions for Defending the Faith
Bahnsen

Bahnsen, Greg
Pushing the Antithesis: The Apologetic Methodology of Greg L. Bahnsen
American Vision Press

Bayly, Lewis
The Practice of Piety
Soli Deo Gloria

DeMar, Gary
Thinking Straight in a Crooked World
AV Press

Hanson, Buddy
Its Time to Un-Quo the Status: How to normalize the present abnormal culture of a non-Christian, upside-down world and turn it rightside up with Christian principles
Hanson Group

Van Til, Cornelius
A Survey of Christian Epistemology
Den Delk Foundation

Williamson, G.I.
Westminster Confession of Faith
P & R Publishing

GOD'S TEN WORDS
Practical Applications from the Ten Commandments

"Why does humanity need God's law?" First and foremost it serves as a mirror to show us as we really are (fallen and filthy in God's sight), not as we may imagine we are (not quite perfect, but not as bad as others). This helps us to recognize our need of repenting and placing our faith in Christ's words and work.

The principles contained in the Ten Commandments provide a prescription for not only stopping our culture's decline, but of restoring it to God's will. Each Commandment includes a section on what civilization was like before the influence of that Commandment, plus a review and practical application. Comments from many of the most respected biblical scholars are included.

CHOOSE THIS DAY
God's Instructions on How to Select Leaders

America needs leaders and Choose This Day gives God's formula for selecting them. The civil government policy-making table, like everything else, belongs to God, not man. It should be noted that we're not umpires who "calls'em as we sees'em" when it comes to making our daily decisions, but rather we're players who follow what our coach (God, through His Word) tells us to do. God's duty is to "call the shots," our duty is to obediently follow His game plan. So for Christians to have a goal of being an equal partner in setting society's policies is to greatly demean God. It is exactly because of our refusal to be "salt and light" to our communities that we have lost not only our seat at culture's table, but the entire table, and getting it back won't be easy. Still, it can be done and as soon as we have secured one seat, we need to begin working on a second seat, and then a third, until we have recaptured them all.

THE CHRISTIAN CIVIL RULER'S HANDBOOK

As important as it is to elect Christian civil rulers (legislators and judges), this is only the first step. Unless the Christians we elect to office have a developed Christian worldview, they will govern no differently than a non-Christian conservative. The Handbook provides a quick read for busy legislators on how to rule according to God's will, instead of according to their own imagination of how God might want them to govern.

Two appendices extend the practical applications discussed in the Handbook. The first one answers common objections regarding religion and politics, and the second one is a multiple choice test on the U.S. Constitution (with an answer key) that Home Schoolers like to use. Get a copy for your Civil Rulers!

THE CHRISTIAN PRINCE
Putting Civil Back into Civil Government

The Christian Prince:
- is the first Christian response to Machiavelli's The Prince in 500 years
- explains how we can put "civil" back into civil government, and how America can once again attract others-focused statesmen to serve as our representatives, instead of the self-centered politicians with whom we are so familiar.
- exposes and contrasts the failing ideas of man with the divinely guaranteed-to-succeed ideas of our Lord, Savior and King, Jesus Christ.

BOTTOM LINE THEOLOGY
A Bible Study Feast for Those Who only have Time for a Sandwich

If Bible study could be thought of as a meal there would be several very wholesome full meals available, complete with veggies, bread and beverage. However, when these lengthy books are boiled down to the bottom line you will find that the biblical principles that they teach and those that BLT teaches are the same, because there is only one Bible! The advantage that BLT offers is that you won't use up most of your time in searching for the biblical principles in which you are interested. So, if your current schedule necessitates that you grab a fast spiritual sandwich, then BLT is the Bible study for you. Each of the thirteen sections gets directly to the heart of the Biblical principles discussed.

FLOWERS FOR THE CHRISTIAN WORLDVIEW GARDEN

Not quite sure what a Christian worldview is? If so, you're not alone. Only one in twenty Christian adults knows the answer. The seven chapters of FLOWERS discuss the various aspects of a developed Christian worldview. All Christians have one or more of these aspects included in their Worldview Garden, but God desires that we have all seven, because the more "flowers" we have, the less "weeds" we will have. The elements of a developed Christian worldview are:

From Him, through Him and to Him are all things. Romans 11.36
Lean not on your own understanding. Proverbs 3.5
Obedience brings blessings. Leviticus 26; Deuteronomy 28
Word of God is true. Psalm 119.160
Exhibit humility. Matthew 23.12
Repent. Ezekiel 14.6
Saved to succeed, not secede. Psalm 2.8

DAILY BLT
A Daily Arsenal of Godly Ammunition to help you Take Ground for God's Kingdom

DAILY BLT is unique in that it gives practical tools to use according to the way that best fits your personality and schedule. Each Day has three 2-page sections, and depending upon your schedule you can use one (15-minutes), two (30 minutes), or all three (45-minutes) of these 2-page sections. Since Sunday is a Sabbath Day Rest in the Lord, fourteen additional pages are provided.

MAKING YOUR DAILY READS: VOL. I, II & III
How to READ the Defense of your Opponents' Objections
to Christianity and Make the Right Call to Uphold the Faith

Making Your Daily READS provides 52 "READS," for the various objections the reader is likely to encounter on a daily basis. The READS are categorized into five "audibles:"

> **R** – One religion is as good as another
> **E** – God doesn't know everything, besides eternity is where Jesus wins
> **A** – Apologetics; defending the faith against common objections
> **D** – God is dead when it comes to "real life" issues.
> **S** – The State is exempt from God's authority.

Each audible begins with a Scouting Report that sets the theme for the section. Following that is one READ for each week with a page for the reader to re-write the READ in their own words, and spend the entire week practicing it. As a bonus, a short course in apologetics is included in an appendix.

THY WILL BE DONE ON EARTH
Heavenly Insights for Down-to-Earth Living
from the Prophet Isaiah

Isaiah's "fifth Gospel" is the most quoted Old Testament book in the New Testament. Isaiah's message offers valuable insights on how to best deal with the situations and circumstances in which we find ourselves. Pastor and author Martyn Lloyd-Jones writes, "[Isaiah] is relevant because it is a book that deals with men and women in their relationships to God ... this is not merely a contemporary message, it is the message of God for the condition of humanity at all times and in all places."

What's Scripture Got To Do With It?
Connecting Your Spiritual Dots for a More Meaningful Life

Every Christian could list core biblical truths in which he unquestionably believes. Unfortunately, few of us incorporate these beliefs into our lifestyle. How is it with you? Does your lifestyle consistently demonstrate the "answers" you say that the Bible has to life's questions? Are you being salt and light to those with whom you come into contact, or has your salt lost its savor, and is good for nothing else but to be trampled under foot?

Many of us have a lot of "Spiritual Dots" (core Christian beliefs) floating around inside our mind that for one reason or another we have not connected to our everyday lifestyle. What's Scripture Got To Do With It? will raise your awareness of those particular Spiritual Dots and stresses the urgency to live in accordance with them.

Its Time to Un-Quo the Status
How to normalize the present abnormal culture of a non-Christian, upside-down world and turn it rightside up with Christian principles

What does being a Christian mean? Should our lifestyle really be different than that of a non-Christian? And what about our culture: Is "tweaking it" a little with Christian values about the best we can expect, or should we strive to completely transform it? It's Time to Un-Quo the Status addresses these issues by discussing four overarching questions:

- Who Are We & What Are We Supposed To Do?
- Should Christians Be Seen & Not Heard?
- How To Take Ground For Christ's Kingdom
- The Absolute & Positive Hope For The Earth

EXIT Strategy
A Handbook to Exponentially Improve Your Service for God

If you've been itching for an antidote for the rampant Spiritual anemia that exists throughout your community, EXIT Strategy provides the scratch. Each reader will be able to evaluate a book they're about to buy, or a study they're thinking of joining with thirteen Door Opener worksheets that quickly identify whether they will be involved in simply another form of church "busyness," or in an activity that will help them grow in their personal holiness.

While every Christian knows we must obey God, EXIT Strategy clarifies that in order to obey God in the way God prefers, we must first know and understand His Word. This is achieved through the exclusive Door Opener worksheets, plus the complete Westminster Larger Catechism (196 questions).

This Is Not A Drill
Real Lessons for Real People from the Real God,
Through His prophets, on how to live and govern ourselves,
Really!

This Is Not A Drill is designed to be a resource book for you and your family (and hopefully even a small group study with your friends). With this in mind, the format has been designed more along that of a textbook, than a novel. To help you understand the historical circumstances to which each prophet is speaking, the content is divided into three sections:
- History & Hypocrisy: Conforming ourselves to the world
- Habits: Reforming ourselves to the Word, and
- Holiness or Holocaust? Blessings or Curses: God's sovereignty in History and Prophecy

Just Because
Jesus Saves You from the Fire
It Doesn't Mean
You Get to Drive the Fire Truck!

How the "Me first" brand of Christianity is in fact "No Christianity" at all, and why our Culture will continue to unravel unless and until we "Seek first the Kingdom of God," (Matthew 6.33) by abandoning the idea of there being a God, and begin dealing with the reality of God and the responsibilities that are connected to being a Christian. Fire Truck assists you in

- Answering the question: "Am I getting the job done, as a Christian?" by explaining what you have been called into Christ's Kingdom to accomplish, and by helping you develop a "vision" of how to live as a Christian. We should not forget that God isn't interested that we know His will, but that we do His will.
- Making the non-negotiable attitude change from "What's in this for me?" to "What's in this for Christ's Kingdom?"
- Exchanging subjective conservative moralism for objective Christian reality.
- Developing the awareness and understanding of how a God-oriented lifestyle is superior to a man-oriented lifestyle.
- Striving for consistency in your Christian walk, not complacency.

Re-examining Your Teaching Paradigm
Expanding your approach from Informant to Instructor by advancing from the current "Listening and Learning" mindset of your congregation to the "Listening, Learning and Doing" mindset

Re-examining Your Teaching Paradigm "repeats" the original approach to the pulpit by the Protestant Reformers, (Puritans), and to some readers this "original approach" may sound so new that they will be tempted to dismiss it. The truth, however, is that what is presented is completely old and proven. Indeed, it was this original way of pastors communicating with their members that helped to "Christianize" the West. Slowly and gradually, pastors have wandered far from the Puritan pulpit model, and as a result, the once solid Christian cultural principles of the West have been replaced by the pluralistic principles from every form of religion except Christianity.

Today's church members are likely to determine the "good guys" in the pulpit from the "bad guys" by how accurate their biblical exegesis is in their sermons. Over the years this zeal to make certain that their members are correctly informed has resulted in a "Listening and Learning" paradigm among Christians, whereby they judge the value of a church according to how solid its teaching is. This paradigm, however, ignores the two most basic questions on the mind of everyone who listens to your sermons:

- What does this message mean for me?
- How should these biblical truths impact my worldview and lifestyle?

Re-examining Your Teaching Paradigm encourages pastors to replace the current "Listening and Learning" paradigm that they are either intentionally or unintentionally presenting to their members, with the "Listening, Learning and Doing" paradigm of their Puritan brothers. As they do this Christians of all ages will be excited to find that they have been called into Christ's Kingdom with a most important purpose, which is to restore our culture to its pre-Fall condition.

How to De-Program Yourself
From all of the Blasphemous Ideas You Learned in Public School

For more than 160 years American educators have been turning out Marxist "Manchurian Candidates," who have been subtly indoctrinated to respond to cultural issues in ungodly ways, all the while thinking that they are "card carrying Christians." The operative word here is "think," and it is the way they have been taught to think (or not think) that is the brilliance of the public (government) school movement, and the shame of Pastors to allow their God to be systematically blasphemed on a daily basis.

If you think that it is beyond the realm of possibilities that your "strings" are being pulled in order for you to make your daily decisions according to the non-Christian worldview cultural agenda that is currently in vogue, read this book F-A-S-T!

RETURN TO SINNER
Are Your Daily Decisions Betraying Your Christian Testimony?

What does it mean to be a Christian?

What is it like to "image" Jesus in what we think, say and do?

What changes need to be made in the worldview and lifestyle of a new
  Christian from the worldview and lifestyle he had before his conversion?

If a non-Christian were to ask any Christian these typical questions, he would likely receive some impressive answers. However, when the non-Christian begins to try to find Christian neighbors who are living according to the answers he receives, he may very well conclude that "all of this town's Christians must have gone on vacation." RETURN describes how to "love the Lord your God with your whole heart," and live your life in a God-honoring manner.

DIVINE COMEBACKS

How many people do you speak to each day? Whether in an office, on the telephone, through email, or on the street, you have countless opportunities to bring honor to Jesus.

What if you could turn every greeting into an opportunity to a non-threatening way to share the gospel?

If this sounds interesting *Divine ComeBacks* could be the most practical book you'll read this year. *Divine ComeBacks* offers you non-threatening biblical responses to common greetings, such as "How are you doing?" "How are things going?" and "What have you been up to since the last time I saw you?" The *Divine ComeBacks* are grouped among five categories which directly relate to everyday situations and circumstances:

- Dominion/Victory
- Lifestyle/Testimony (Holiness)
- Confident/Optimistic Attitude
- Worldview/Faith
- Consistent Obedience to God's Word

Today is a good day to begin greeting your Christian friends and non-Christian neighbors with a non-threatening, yet convicting *Divine ComeBack*!

NOW THAT YOU'RE A CHRISTIAN
How and Why You Should Bring Glory and Honor
To God in Everything You Think, Say and Do

The goal of *Now That You're A Christian* is to guide you in answering the many questions that are common to those who are new to the faith. The various elements of a Christian lifestyle are arranged under the following eight topics:

- The Absolute Superiority of Christianity
- The Absolute Supremacy of Our Triune God
- The Absolute Supremacy of God's Word
- The Superiority of Your Purpose in Life
- The Superiority of the Christian Worldview & Lifestyle
- Your Labor Is Not In Vain in the Lord
- The Spiritual Superiority of Being a Member of God's Family
- What You Can Do Today to Bring Honor to Your Lord,
  Savior and King, Jesus Christ

BUDDY HANSON, President of the Christian Policy Network, and Director of the Christian Worldview Resources Center frequently speaks to Churches Homeschool organizations and civic groups about the necessity of applying biblical principles to every situations, circumstances and decision-making. "There are many fine organizations presenting the descriptions about how a Christian worldview should differ from a non-Christian one, but that's only half of the equation. Our focus is to present God's prescriptions to reform our culture. Christianity is not an intellectual trip, but a world-transforming trip as Jesus commands us to live-out our faith and bring about 'God's will on earth as it is in heaven.'" (Matthew 6.10)

For pricing and ordering information contact:*
The Hanson Group
2 Windsor Drive, Tuscaloosa, Alabama 35404
bhanson@graceandlaw.com • 205.454.1442

Bookstores can also order through Ingram Distributors

* Quantity discounts available

Printed in the United States
107631LV00002B/31-100/P